Praise for *Str*
and Culture for Nonprofits

"Ken is a visionary leader who shares his successful approach to strategic planning in a simple and effective way. As a leader of a non-profit organization whose values drive everything we do, I found Ken's book to be incredibly powerful and helpful in our planning."

— Karen A. Santilli, President & CEO,
Crossroads Rhode Island, helping homeless
or at-risk individuals and families secure stable homes

"Ken has decades of wisdom to share from his experience with some of the world's most highly respected NGOs, and this book is full of wisdom. He approaches topics like strategic planning and organization culture from a high level and then dives deep, providing templates and taking readers through exercises to create their own. As a former leader of a youth-led organization, I wish I had something like this to read before preparing for a five-day strategic planning retreat! I recommend this book to any leader with the aspirations to make a difference in their organization and the world."

— Ian Kawetschanky, former President & CEO,
AIESEC United States

"Ken Phillips guided me through multiple strategic plans with a national nonprofit organization that I led for fourteen years. Several strategy sessions were extraordinarily complicated with changing staff, difficult financial challenges, and major organizational transfor-mation. The new strategic plans were critical to the long-term success of the organization. Ken's planning process helped us become a more healthy, sustainably funded organization and helped me grow as a leader. The tools he shared and the process he employed remain with me today. I'm forever indebted to Ken for his deep passion for non-profit success."

– Rebecca Morley, former Executive Director,
National Center for Healthy Housing

"Ken Phillips covers all the ABCs of doing strategic planning as well as operating plans. He writes in a detailed fashion about the rationale for good planning and then provides the how-to process to do it."

– William Reese, former CEO,
International Youth Foundation, USA

"As a visionary and fearless leader in empowering nonprofits to reach their full potential, Ken was instrumental to NYC Kids Project's birth and growth. Ken guided us to establish our organizational backbone of vision and mission at the early stage and continued to challenge and inspire us to think bigger and reach higher as we thrived. In the meantime, he equipped us with tools for success through his expertise in fundraising and connections as we grew from zero to impacting thousands of children in New York City today."

– Nell Mei, former Board Chair,
New York City Kids Project

"Working with Ken was a lasting course in strategic planning. When moving on to other national and international organizations, those strategic planning skills prepared me for unimaginable challenges. Each time, I had the right tools to lead others in building a better society – from programs addressing U.S. child welfare systemic needs at the helm of two U.S. national organizations to leading international child-labor elimination programs and human rights work as CEO of a private foundation in Switzerland to my current work leading local programs for youth. In each leadership position, I have partnered with a local board and engaged loyal individuals and foundations. Each endeavor started with the foundational strategic planning approach I learned with Ken. Thank you, Ken, for this new book and for your amazing legacy in this field!"

– Sonia C. Velazquez, Executive Director,
Literature for All of Us, Chicago

"We have worked with Ken Phillips in various formats. For our Down syndrome organization, he led a three-day strategic session where we crystallized the mission of the organization, understanding of its role, and the direction for development. We also had the opportunity to provide fundraising training for our regional representatives. This training has enabled several oblast organizations to start self-financing their programs and has been an impetus for the development of services for children with Down syndrome and their families across Ukraine."

– Tatiana Mikhailenko, Vice President of the European Down
Syndrome Association, International Liaison Coordinator,
Ukrainian Charitable Down Syndrome Organization

"As a founder of a nonprofit in Nigeria, it has been particularly difficult to get adequate funding for all our projects and activities. This book has helped introduce me to the importance of strategic planning and how it can bring about sustainability within our organization. It also outlines practical ways to get all stakeholders within an organization involved in strategic planning, along with practical examples of organizations that have used this approach. I recommend this book for NGO leaders around the world. I believe it will help enhance our passion and enable us to achieve better outcomes."

– Titilayo Ogunbambi, Founder/Executive Director,
Boundless Hands Africa Initiative, Nigeria

Strategic Planning and Culture for Nonprofits

Clear and doable steps to create motivating plans and the supporting culture you need for success

The six books in Ken Phillips' Civil Society Series are:

1. *Make a Better World: A practical guide to leadership and fundraising success: Raise more money and have greater impact through strategy, teamwork, and stepping up*
2. *Strategic Planning and Culture for Nonprofits: Clear and doable steps to create motivating plans and the supporting culture you need for success*
3. *25 Proven Strategies for Fundraising Success: How to win the love and support of donors*
4. *Ethics and Learning for Trustworthiness: Two essential priorities to gain the trust of donors*
5. *Governance, Management, and Teams: Everyone working together for effectiveness*
6. *Advocating for Civil Society and Philanthropy: Mobilizing a social movement*

Strategic Planning and Culture for Nonprofits: Clear and doable steps to create motivating plans and the supporting culture you need for success

Book Two in the Civil Society Series
By Ken Phillips

Copyright © 2021 by Ken Phillips, NGO Futures LLC

All rights reserved. The text of this publication, or any part thereof, may not be reproduced in any manner whatsoever without written permission from the author.

This book is for general informational purposes only. It does not provide specific legal advice and should not be relied on as such. The author does not guarantee that the information in this book will produce certain financial results for individuals or any type of organization or association. The material is general in nature and cannot substitute for customized professional advice. Any trade name or product name mentioned is property of its respective owner. Further, the author is not liable if the reader relied on the material and was financially damaged in some way. Any statements about the recollection of stories shared are recalled to the best of the author's knowledge.

Published by
NGO Futures LLC
www.NGOFutures.com
NGOFutures@gmail.com

Library of Congress Cataloging-in-Publication Data
Phillips, Ken
Strategic Planning and Culture for Nonprofits: Clear and doable steps to create motivating plans and the supporting culture you need for success

ISBN: 978-1-7923-3136-7 (softcover)
Library of Congress Control Number: 2020917203
First Edition
Printed in the United States of America

Working Together for a Better World

Through Strategy, Teamwork, and Leadership

I dedicate this book to the visionary entrepreneurs working as leaders, managers, and fundraisers for nonprofit organizations and community groups around the world who are achieving progress and improvements for so many people in need and for the planet. They taught me so much of what I present here. They are truly at the top of the pyramid of human values, which I presented in the first book in this series as a fundamental principle in fundraising and social development.

NGO board members, staff, and volunteers throughout the world are helping their societies move from a culture of consumerism to a culture of caring and helping others. They all deserve our dedication and support.

Hierarchy of Human Values

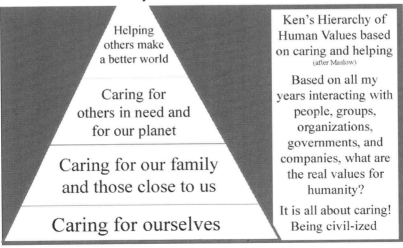

Helping others make a better world

Caring for others in need and for our planet

Caring for our family and those close to us

Caring for ourselves

Ken's Hierarchy of Human Values based on caring and helping (after Maslow)

Based on all my years interacting with people, groups, organizations, governments, and companies, what are the real values for humanity?

It is all about caring! Being civil-ized

Acknowledgments

I acknowledge with joy all those individuals over the years who have guided and assisted me in developing the content and substance for this book and succeeding books in my Civil Society Series – and more recently praise for Sara Neagu and Rosa Morales for their gracious work on translations of my first book into Romanian and Spanish, Patrice Rhoades-Baum for advice and editing for this book, Sawyer Phillips for his amazing cartoons, Sonia Velazquez and Steve Sookikian for profound insights that I now include here, and finally four amazing young interns who have helped during the summer of 2020: Molly Davis, Isha Ganapathiraju, Haru Nishigaki, and Natalie Song. They believe in the Sustainable Development Goals, the power of dreams, and their ability to make dreams come true to make a better world.

The Challenge to NGOs to Step Up

CONTENTS

Preface

Thank you for building a more civil society!

Are you an executive director, fundraising or program director, team member, volunteer, or board member in a nonprofit organization, community association, or group in formation? If so, thank you! Whether your organization focuses on children, housing, education, animal welfare, the environment, or any other worthwhile cause, you are joining people like me and many millions of others around the globe who are actively working to build a more civil society.

This book is the second in my comprehensive *Civil Society Series* on how to make this a better world. The series will empower you to make real change for the better. The guidance in this book presents the steps to create a realistic strategic and operational plan, so you will become a stronger and more sustainable organization.

An article in the *Guardian*, a leading British newspaper, reported a survey in August 2020 that "Almost half of U.K. charities for the world's poorest [are] set to close in a year" due to lack of financial support during the COVID-19 crisis. But this would not need to happen if all these nonprofits had good strategic plans and supporting organization culture!

Throughout this series, I use the terms *organizations, nonprofits,* and *NGOs* (non-governmental organizations) as the broadest terms to cover legally registered nonprofit organizations or charities, established community organizations, professional associations, and informal groups that are formed for the public benefit. These types of organizations comprise the civil society sector.

A vigorous civil society sector is critical

As I noted in my first book, a vigorous civil society sector is essential for the wellbeing of society. The civil society sector consists of a wide variety of charitable nonprofit organizations and associations dedicated to making some aspect of the world better. Civil society organizations encourage people to act on their best impulses to help others by donating funds and volunteering their time. This describes the phenomenon of people coming together to do something worthwhile for the good of society – without the motive of personal profit.

A well-functioning civil society is where:

- Every individual enjoys the freedom to create a group or organization to take steps to make society better.
- Government facilitates the creation of organizations dedicated to the public good and allows freedom of assembly, speech, and association.
- Neighbors, businesses, authorities, and others have a commitment at the community level to take steps to improve the conditions surrounding them in health, education, safety, environment, support, and other conditions for a high-quality life.
- Individuals, corporations, governments, and other institutions donate money, time, and materials, as appropriate, to help people who are sick, homeless, impoverished, or held back by disasters, handicaps, health, lack of education, or any other barrier.
- Individuals, organizations, and institutions work together to protect all members of society through environmental

action, justice for all, equal opportunity, gender equality, and other universal human rights.

- Individuals, organizations, and other institutions provide information, education, and advocacy to assure good behavior by government, corporations, and organizations.

These are the conditions that make a society civil and that make life for all more harmonious. To help create these conditions, civil society organizations – nonprofits, community associations, and new groups – need to build their capacity, raise more funds, and achieve more impact.

You can help build a more civil society by stepping up as a leader, no matter who you are!

Underlying all I have written is the conviction that leaders can operate at all levels of an organization and in all areas of society. Few of us will be historic leaders, but most of us can lead from where we are right now in our society, in our community, and in our work.

Whether you are an executive director, fundraising or program director, other staff member, volunteer, or board member, this book is a useful tool, guiding you to lead your organization's strategic planning process. A realistic (but stretching) strategic plan will empower your organization to achieve a greater impact and make our world a better place. If you are not already involved in a nonprofit, you can join or even create a nonprofit group in your neighborhood or community. You can be an effective change agent. The guidance, examples, and worksheets in this book will help you achieve the changes you want to make. *I believe you can do it!*

This is a guidebook to enable you to plan, organize, implement, and follow a strategic plan and supporting strategies, just like the best

NGOs. After an introduction on the power of strategic planning, this book follows a logical progression: first an overview to provide understanding of strategic and operational planning and understanding of core values and organization culture (Parts I and II). Next, you get step-by-step guidance to create your strategic and operational plans, clarify and confirm your core values, and create the new, desired organization culture (Parts III and IV). Finally, Part V addresses after-the-planning actions with advice for implementation.

The four appendices offer useful tools: a checklist to identify what needs to be done in your strategic plan, considerations to prepare for your strategic planning retreat, a template agenda for a three-day planning retreat, and instructions to access and download a complete packet of detailed worksheets from www.NGOFutures.com to use during your planning sessions. These worksheets are important items to use during the actual planning, since participants can use them in the step-by-step process in their individual and group work.

The six books in my *Civil Society Series* are specially created for nonprofit organizations, professional associations, and community groups that seek grants, donations, and volunteer support to do their valuable good works. These organizations and any volunteer work you do comprise an important civil society sector. Whether you are an executive director, fundraiser, team member, volunteer, or board member in your organization, you are building a more civil society. Thank you!

Introduction

The power of strategic planning

The first formal strategic plan I created was when I worked as director of fundraising at Save the Children in the United States. At the time, it was a small and unknown organization. Soon after taking this position, I realized the fundraising effort did not receive enough support from the rest of the organization. Plus, it seemed the executive director and I continually needed to discuss specific strategies, objectives, and tactics for every individual fundraising project or marketing effort. These internal debates took time (and led to a certain amount of frustration) to get on the same page, make decisions, and keep moving forward.

I decided to lead a planning process to guide the organization to create its first strategic plan with a focus on fundraising. This enlightening and teambuilding process helped to align the leadership team by discussing expectations and agreeing to underlying strategies. Having a strategic plan – agreed upon by all of us in top management – enabled me to fully take control of my fundraising activities. Now armed with an approved strategic plan, I could weave through challenges and take advantage of opportunities. It gave me the basis to secure the support I needed from other departments as well as the strategy to manage the fundraising effort. Plus, I did not receive as many phone calls from my boss on weekends.

Results of the strategic planning included a new logo and vastly improved branding, a significant increase in public awareness, expanded volunteer support, development of a profitable craft center with proceeds for children, new program strategy that was more effective in the field and more appealing to donors, better reports on results from the program offices, widespread support by board and staff for new marketing and public relations ventures, and substantial, ongoing increases in revenues.

Clearly, with increased fundraising results, we were able to help many more children, their families, and communities. Equally important, the strategic planning laid the groundwork for decades to come with further diversification of revenues, sustainability, a strong national reputation, global program development that helps far more children and families, and leadership in civil society.

Years later in my consulting business, as another example, I was retained by a large NGO in Switzerland to develop its strategic fundraising plan, which involved all staff and board members in supporting fundraising. The planning process proved to be extremely successful. When I first engaged with the organization, its annual revenue was $5 million. Just three years later, this NGO's annual revenue grew to $20 million. When I visited the office ten years later I was greeted by a standing round of applause. Revenue had skyrocketed to $60 million! *This is the power of strategic planning.*

This book will guide you to create (and implement) your on-target strategic plan

While working with a very large international organization with many national affiliates, I discovered that while all the affiliates had comprehensive strategic plans, many of them had simply filed the plan after its completion. These plans were not living documents that continuously guided the organization. What happened? The plans had been drafted by outside consultants who failed to understand local realities or get enough local involvement. The resulting plans were not relevant, based in reality, or much used. The key is to use a *participatory* process to create a reality-based strategic plan that will inspire and guide everyone in your organization for the next three (or five) years.

Whether you are the executive director, fundraising director, other director, or any other staff member, you can step up to lead this process. You and your team can create a robust strategic plan that is truly strategic and reality-based, along with supporting operational plans. While this is a large task, it is not an impossible one. Clearly, I believe it is absolutely critical for your organization to create – and follow – a strategic plan.

A 2019 survey by The Concord Leadership Group found that half of nonprofits in the United States did not have a strategic plan at all or have one that they were not following. I was astounded to read this and troubled to think how these organizations are managed.

In this book, I provide a roadmap to overcome that failure and to strengthen the plans for all nonprofits that are not satisfied with their results.

This book describes how to draft a strong strategic plan and operational plans as well as create strong values and a new, desired culture to support fundraising, program, and other functions in your organization. I urge you to use this approach whether your organization is a nonprofit with paid staff, an all-volunteer organization, and even a new group in formation. The all-volunteer organization is in some ways as complicated as the one with paid staff, so all components of planning are relevant to both. Groups that are newly formed need to address all of this in their planning and organizing and can do so in a simplified manner.

As you prepare for your strategic planning process, keep these points in mind:

- The two main goals of this book are to (1) help your organization create a three-year (or five-year) strategic plan as well as supporting operational plans for each functional area such as fundraising, program, and finance/administration; and (2) create strong values and a new, desired organization culture that will support the implementation of your strategic plan and help ensure you successfully reach your goals.

- The strategic planning process I present is a doable process for any nonprofit organization, community association, or even a new group of concerned neighbors, whether the group is small or large. It is not that difficult to do!

- This is a surprisingly fast, efficient process honed from my many decades as fundraiser and executive in nonprofit organizations and as consultant and trainer for numerous NGOs around the world. Most NGOs can complete this planning process in a three-day retreat after sufficient research has been completed. Some groups can complete this process during several meetings.

- The resulting plans are not hefty, burdensome documents. They are relatively brief and, ideally, extremely inspiring and exciting for all stakeholders including staff, board members, volunteers, and donors – even for program participants or beneficiaries!

- A strategic plan is not just a set of goals, but it is the pathway to develop, thrive, and achieve the results you want. Also, the planning process is a necessary way to

generate focus and commitment by everyone involved.
You will be amazed by the results!

Throughout my career, I came to appreciate the importance of the critical planning components – vision, mission, core values, strategic goals, key strategies, positioning, trustworthiness, and organization culture – to create a realistic (yet stretching) strategic plan. You can download and share detailed worksheets and additional tools at my website to use in the actual planning (www.NGOFutures.com). The worksheets, which I always use in planning sessions with clients around the world, will make the job of leading the planning easy to do.

As you read the following chapters, I encourage you to take notes, complete the worksheets in this book, and write down your ideas and inspiration. Your newly created strategic plan and operational plans will direct your organization into the future. They will guide your staff, volunteers, and other stakeholder to achieve ever-greater accomplishments. With on-target plans, your nonprofit or community organization can make an even greater impact.

Read Parts I and II for a more complete understanding of strategic and operational planning and values and culture. Use Parts III and IV to lead the actual drafting of the strategic plan, operational plans, strong values, and organization culture. Follow Part V to complete the planning process. Download detailed worksheets and other tools free from my website, www.NGOFutures.com.

A good catch is rarely a coincidence.

PART I

Understanding strategic and operational planning – 10,000 foot view

Which statement best describes your organization?

- "I know where I want our organization to go and how to do it. Everyone just has to follow me."
- "We involved everyone in our planning process, we have an exciting plan, and everyone is motivated."

Without question, completing an on-target, inspiring strategic plan will empower your organization to say: "We involved everyone in our planning process, we have an exciting plan, and everyone is motivated." Better yet, your team will be more likely to meet realistic (yet stretching) goals!

To begin thinking about your strategic planning process, it is helpful to have a "bird's-eye view" of the overall process. Here are the key steps presented in this book – and how all the pieces fit together:

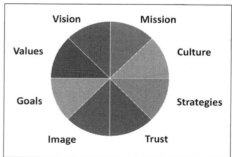

1. *Vision* for a better world that inspires others to join you in your shared dreams
2. *Mission* that empowers everyone to move the vision to desired results
3. *Core values* that you believe most deeply as the fundamentals that guide you in everything
4. *Strategic goals* that you must achieve in three to five years to succeed in your work

5. *Key strategies* as "how" to reach your goals and objectives and to meet stakeholder needs
6. *Positioning* to clarify how others see your organization – different, special, and appealing
7. *Trustworthiness* or *credibility* as essential attributes – why people should trust you
8. *Organization culture* so you behave and work together for success

Together, these eight elements constitute your new strategic directions and form a perfect unity for your organization. With this foundation, your organization will create strategic and operational plans that are clear, doable, and realistic. I believe you will find, as so many others have found, that my step-by-step process is uplifting and energizing. By following this process, your organization's realistic (yet stretching) strategic and operational plans will be truly inspiring documents, based in reality and creativity.

When I was president and national executive director of Foster Parents Plan (now called PLAN International USA), we tripled donations from $10 million to $30 million ($64 million in today's value), reduced administrative staff by 25 percent, initiated and secured major changes and improvements in board leadership and membership, established a prestigious honorary board, and initiated effective educational and advocacy programs. All of this came about as a result of good strategic planning. I'll share more about this later in the book. Keep reading to learn how your organization can make a greater impact!

Whether you are the nonprofit's executive director, fundraising director, program director, staff member, or board member, you can step up to lead this process. You can involve others to create strategic, living documents that will guide everyone in your organization to reach clearly defined goals and objectives – and make a greater impact. (See my first book to learn more about how you can step up to lead in important ways even when you are not "the boss.")

The next three chapters cover what you must understand and the research you need to complete before implementing the actual strategic and operational planning.

1

What is strategic management for a nonprofit organization?

Anonprofit organization needs to be smart in what it does, how it behaves, and how it communicates. Strategic management is doing everything within the organization *strategically* – thinking strategically all the time, planning strategically for your future, acting strategically month to month and even day to day, and evaluating strategically what it does to achieve its key goals and objectives. In a strategic organization, every function – program, fundraising, finance, and administration – is pulling in the same direction to achieve strategic results, and everyone is involved in supporting fundraising.

The work of a nonprofit flows from support by donors through the organization with its objectives, activities, and strategies to achieve results for participants and society. When I speak of donors, I include donors of money and time. Both are giving your organization something that is valuable to you as well as to themselves.

The strategic plan identifies the organization's vision, mission, values, and goals along with its positioning and trustworthiness in the marketplace. Having the right organization culture enables everyone to work together smoothly to achieve the best possible results for participants and society. *Culture underlies everything.*

A good strategic plan is based on a deep awareness of reality resulting from research, a SWOT analysis (assessment of internal *strengths* and *weaknesses* and external *opportunities* and *threats*), and

Strategic Management

a clear understanding of critical success factors, along with creativity and innovation. This is *strategic management*. This is the model I have personally implemented at several nonprofit organizations and then taught around the world, and it is the model presented here.

After a brief discussion about the importance of strategic thinking and creating a high-level strategy, this book offers detailed advice to move forward with your strategic plan and operational plans, along with key steps to complete your planning process. The strategic plan describes the big ideas, and the operational plans describe their implementation. In other words, the operational plans detail the exact steps you choose to achieve objectives. The final essential part of planning we cover is identifying and creating the culture you need to support your goals and objectives.

Developing the strategic plan and culture should be based on a good understanding of *Make a Better World: A practical guide to leadership and fundraising success* (the first book in my *Civil Society Series*). After you complete your strategic plan and instill your new, desired culture, you can address the next essential topics to strengthen your organization, which are covered in my forthcoming books: *25 Proven Strategies for Fundraising Success; Ethics and Learning for Trustworthiness; Governance, Management, and Teams; and Advocating for Civil Society and Philanthropy*. Underlying everything is the importance of activating leadership at all levels to assure the organization has the capacity needed for success.

What is strategic thinking?

We need to address *strategic thinking* first. The word *strategic* refers to the big picture, the highest level of thinking, the longest term, and the overall framework for your planning and daily work. The word *thinking* refers to the highest level of human performance.

René Descartes wrote: "Cogito, ergo sum!" or "I think; therefore I am." In all the processes for nonprofits, strategic thinking is required. But I also say: "*Ducéo, ergo cogito!* ("I lead, therefore I think!")

Pedestrian thinking or trend thinking will give you "small thoughts" and a low level of achievement. The leaders of an organization are responsible to assure that strategic thinking is brought into play at all levels and by everyone involved. This especially includes the fundraisers who are in contact with the people and institutions who give you money.

The *Competency Framework* created by the Organisation for Economic Co-operation and Development (OECD) goes to the heart of responsibility in nonprofits. It defines strategic thinking as "the ability to develop a broad, big-picture view of the Organisation and its mission. Competitive advantage and threats, industry trends, emerging technology, market opportunities, stakeholder focus – Strategic Thinking is where these all come together. Strategic Thinking keeps individuals and groups focused and helps decide where to invest critical resources. It includes the ability to link long-range visions and concepts to daily work."

The first step to create an effective nonprofit organization is to have a powerful sense of purpose. The sense of purpose is generally contained in two organizational statements – its *vision* (why you exist) and its *mission* (what you do to achieve that vision).

The vision is inspiring and the mission is empowering, so these two statements inspire and empower staff, volunteers, and donors. They unify everyone in common pursuit of what you want your organization to accomplish.

The vision statement describes the ideal world you want to see for those whom you serve. The vision for a child-focused organization, for example, could be "a world in which all children are healthy, educated, active, and happy." The mission statement describes whom you serve, what needs you meet, and how you achieve the results you want. It reflects and contributes to the organization's vision. The mission statement for that child-focused organization could be "to provide healthcare, educational support, sports, art, and family counseling." Vision and mission statements are clear, brief, and memorable.

The nonprofit's strategic plan is similar to a business plan, with critical differences

The differences between businesses and nonprofit organizations are profound. The business model defines how to make money, while the nonprofit's strategic plan defines how to benefit society. The value proposition for companies is in the products or services people will buy, while the value proposition for nonprofits is in their vision and

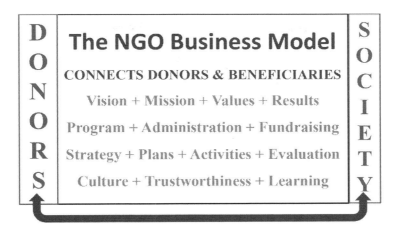

mission statements and the call to action to contribute to make this a better world.

Whereas companies attract customers to buy sausages, stocks, subscriptions, sweaters, or other things usually for their own use and benefit, nonprofits ask people to give their money or time to make a better world by helping hungry children, impoverished communities, tsunami victims, or abused animals or by supporting cultural institutions, youth programs, anticorruption efforts, environmental activities, or other broad social issues.

In their business model, companies attract *stockholders* by promising a profit, while in their strategic plans, nonprofits attract *stakeholders* by promising a better world. A nonprofit's stakeholders care about other people and the world we live in, which is a more complex concept than what customers or stockholders care about for a business.

Also, the revenue model for nonprofits is more complicated than the model for most businesses, because nonprofits generate resources from one set of stakeholders (donors) to provide benefits to an entirely different set of stakeholders (beneficiaries or program participants). Of course, many companies also care about the world we live in, but this is not a concept firmly baked into current business theory and practice.

For nonprofit organizations, the fundamental issue of raising money from donors to provide services to others is the biggest challenge. To succeed, of course, it is necessary to have an effective program that delivers results. The business model for a nonprofit is, in simple terms, to find a way (a plan or strategy) to inspire people to help others by donating their time or money for the cause and, as a means to do this, to have an effective, efficient, and trusted organization that delivers meaningful results. This requires providing value and benefits to the organization's beneficiaries and, at the same time, providing value and benefits to donors and volunteers.

The time to plan your future is now

If you don't have a strong strategic plan in place, now is the best time to launch the process. Delaying this will mean you are just "going with the flow" without making the effort to think strategically about your organization's future and how you want to guide it.

An organization needs a strategic plan that:

- Gives direction for its activities and services
- Assures an effective program and efficient management
- Attracts support from external stakeholders
- Guides everyone in their work – what you want to do, how you will achieve it, and how everyone can help

The needs in the world are so pressing that all nonprofits should strive to do more as long as they are operating effectively, efficiently, ethically, and accountably. Anyone who questions the need for more such activities can look at the United Nation's Sustainable Development Goals adopted by 193 governments in 2015 as the global agenda

What Is the Future?

◆ Today's choices determine tomorrow's results.
◆ Organizations that don't grow die!!

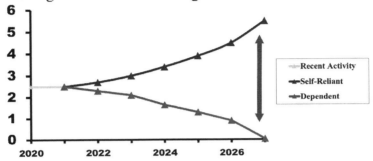

for progress and development. The Sustainable Development Goals represent the pressing fundraising challenge for all organizations to do more and do it better!

No matter what position you hold in your nonprofit or association, you can decide to grow and develop your organization or you can decide to do nothing. The choice between deciding (growth) and not deciding (withering away) is up to you.

Today, most nonprofits have a *strategic plan for the program* they deliver that:

1. Defines who and how you want to help
2. Measures results to confirm you are doing it well
3. Monitors progress and makes corrections when needed
4. Tests your program strategy to assure you are helping effectively
5. Involves participants or representatives in planning, implementation, and evaluation

A *strategic plan for fundraising* is just as important. The strategic plan for fundraising:

1. Involves new donors and raises more money
2. Earns public trust through reliability, good behavior, and accountability
3. Enables the organization to become well known among potential donors
4. Assures donors you are using resources efficiently and achieving good results
5. Identifies and develops important and appealing issues, so your nonprofit is attractive to donors

And it is important to have a *strategic plan for finance and administration* that:

1. Assures excellent financial budgeting, management, and reporting
2. Supports an organization culture that underlies successful performance
3. Manages an effective volunteer program that increases efficiency and impact
4. Undertakes regular performance reviews and supports talent development of all staff
5. Analyzes costs and manages cost control that does not hinder effectiveness and results

Finally, every nonprofit needs a good *strategic plan for the overall organization* that:

1. Promotes interdepartmental sharing and support
2. Enables the organization to take more control of events
3. Gives everyone the same powerful story to share with others
4. Focuses on the most important issues for everyone's attention

5. Unifies everyone to work together as board members, managers, staff, and volunteers

A *supporting culture* for your organization is also necessary for success that:

1. Assesses and confirms strong core values
2. Designs a new, desired organization culture
3. Identifies potential barriers to the new culture
4. Plans the actions to overcome potential barriers
5. Deploys values and culture in program, advocacy, and public outreach

A well-drafted strategic plan consolidates all the above benefits into a document that is inspiring, clear, comprehensive, and concise. It should be available and understandable for internal and external stakeholders. It is brief, not lengthy – more like a poem than a novel. Substance and brevity are both important.

At a workshop with national affiliates of the World Wildlife Federation, I opened the session by emphasizing that the benefits of strategic planning include thinking ahead, so you can know what to do to get to your destination, establishing a clear focus, getting everyone to pull in the same direction, eliminating least-effective activities, reducing surprises ("firefighting"), agreeing on indicators of progress, and using donations and grants in the best possible ways. I stressed that as an organization gets bigger and more complex, increased interdepartmental communications and coordination become more important. In both planning and implementation, it is wise to recognize that the staff who are most involved in processes and activities are in the best position to identify problems and opportunities for improvement. This is all part of getting organized, taking stock, learning from each other, and engaging the whole team in defining where you want to go and how you will get there.

Investing the necessary time to do a complete strategic plan and operational plans will pay dividends. In the example mentioned in the Introduction, I was retained by Medicines for Malaria Venture in Geneva, Switzerland, to help them develop its fundraising and related organizational development plan. A major global consulting company had drafted an excellent business model for this organization's work in developing antimalarial medicines, but the plan failed to include a good fundraising plan.

Fundraising is more than just raising money. It is making sure your organization earns or warrants the support from donors. Every unit of an organization needs a fundraising component in its strategic and operational planning, because everyone working together in support of fundraising will make your organization attractive to donors, help raise more money, and empower your nonprofit to do more good work.

Working together with the organization's board and staff, we developed a strategic fundraising plan and defined the new, desired culture, which would involve all staff in supporting fundraising. Subsequently, board members became involved in fundraising, program staff identified potential donors at professional conferences, finance supported the investment in fundraising, and fundraisers found more effective messages for major donors. Annual revenues skyrocketed from $5 million to $60 million in less than ten years. This is the power of strategic planning – with a focus on ensuring every part of your organization has a fundraising component in its strategic and operational planning. Without a doubt, everyone working together in support of fundraising will help to raise more money.

When the Swedish Agency for International Development decided to terminate financial support for NGOs in Eastern and Central Europe, they asked me to present two keynotes to guide their NGO recipients to create diversified fundraising strategies. When the United Nations Family Planning Association wanted to develop a completely new multimillion-dollar revenue stream, they asked me to facilitate the process. In both cases, my most important message was the value of strategic planning to get you where you really want to be.

As part of my work with the Red Cross, in conjunction with the Federation and the International Committee of the Red Cross (ICRC), I directed a global team that developed "A Common Approach" to development for the 191 Red Cross and Red Crescent National Societies. The common approach unified IFRC and ICRC in their support for organizational development and capacity building of National Societies including a comprehensive guide to strategy and planning, stages and indicators of development, technical guidance on numerous topics, and profiles and job descriptions for experts in planning. This overall approach was agreed by both the Federation and the ICRC, approved by the Federation's board of directors, and then ratified by the global Red Cross Congress, which brings together all components of the International Red Cross and Red Crescent Movement. This strategic planning provided the basis for further development and evaluation of National Societies for excellent performance.

Strategic planning is the foundational step to grow, develop, and have more impact. Also, it is important to note that I was able to initiate a strategic planning process when I held various roles in different organizations – either as a fundraiser or the executive director. You do not have to be "the boss" to lead this vital process.

Questions for implementation

1. Does your organization currently have a vision statement, mission statement, and core values statement? If so, can they meet the challenges facing you today? Can you find other reports, documents, and analysis in your organization that may be helpful as you think about your organization's strategic planning process?

2. If you already have a strategic plan, are you (or a particular department) having difficulties that the plan fails to address? Is it time to begin the process to develop a new plan for the next three to five years? Are you fully satisfied with your nonprofit's growth and development?

3. Have you promoted the idea of pursuing a strategic planning process with other leaders and managers (at all levels) in your organization? What can you do now – at this stage – to get other internal thought leaders to think positively and energetically about embarking on this planning process?

4. Can you identify other cheerleaders and champions who will support you as you initiate the strategic planning process? How can you get these people on the same page so that, together, you will have a stronger voice to initiate, pursue, and complete the process?

2

Steps to create your strategic and operational plans – Overview

If you are working all by yourself, you may not need a strategic plan, since you may be able to keep some type of plan in your head – and no one else needs to know the intricacies of your plan. But once you add staff, board members, and volunteers, a clear and compelling plan is essential to involve and communicate what you want to do, how you will do it, and what everyone should do to support these goals and objectives.

For example, when I am working alone as a writer or consultant, I know the plans, activities, deadlines, and responsibilities all by myself. As soon as I involve colleagues in my work, it is imperative to develop and share information on plans, activities, deadlines, and responsibilities, so we can coordinate and work together to achieve the desired results.

> *It takes* **team** + work *to succeed in nonprofit work as well as in sports! That's why my slogan is "Working together for a better world through strategy, teamwork, and stepping up."*

On a successful football team, as a further illustration, it is the coach's job to put together the game plan based on experience, research, and optimism. All the players need to know the plans, the strategy, their responsibilities, and the ways of working together to win.

If possible, engage an independent consultant to guide the planning process by laying the foundation for a successful planning retreat, which will yield a robust strategic plan and effective operational plans. In addition to guiding the process, the independent consultant can conduct the confidential interviews and facilitate all preparatory sessions as well as the retreat itself.

Alternatively, find a qualified volunteer or staff member to act as the consultant or facilitator. In either option, this individual should be respected and independent enough to secure candid input in the research while possessing the experience and skills to guide and facilitate the process to get effective participation. The challenge for the organization's leadership is to think strategically and to be open to new information, even if it is critical or negative, to plan the organization's future. A skilled facilitator will make the research and planning flow better. In the rest of this book, I refer to the person filling these responsibilities as the *consultant*, whether he or she is an internal or external facilitator.

Know the four levels of planning

In this book, we will take time to step through these critical levels of planning:

- Strategic planning
- Operational planning
- Culture design
- Organization development

It is important to know the different steps that are involved in planning and to set and keep to an agreed timeline to complete each step in the process. For a typical nonprofit, a few months are usually needed for the research effort prior to the strategic planning retreat. The key strategic planning activities can be completed in a three-day retreat. A community organization may require just a series of meetings with its members and other stakeholders to move through the strategic planning process. More guidance and examples are presented later in this book.

Step 1: Prepare for the process by conducting the needed research before the planning

The *inputs* to a good strategic planning process are leadership, organization, research, facilitation, participants, time, and process. The immediate *outputs* are the written strategic plan and operational plans for the coming period. The long-term *outcomes* include more committed staff and better, more strategic work. The *results* are better program impacts, increased fundraising numbers, and a more efficient organization. As you plan, please remember the flow of inputs to outputs to outcomes to results.

Strategic plans in most organizations are for three years and, in very large organizations with experience in planning, for five years. The first step is to think about the planning process:

- Who should be on the organizing team to prepare and organize the planning?
- What planning methods, facilitation, support, and reporting should you have?
- Who should participate in the preparatory sessions and in the strategic planning itself?
- What research do you need to conduct before the retreat, and who will do it?

Recommended research includes a review of your history, lessons learned from past evaluations and reports, surveys of stakeholder groups, competitor and partner assessments, preliminary donor assessments, analysis by key department directors, confidential interviews with key stakeholders, recommendations by a consultant (internal or external), and assessment of the current strategic plan.

A useful process is to complete Appendix 1 (What needs to be done in your strategic plan?) and to review Appendix 2 (Considerations to prepare for your strategic planning). Your answers will help you determine your process and priorities for the planning.

These preparatory steps will produce a well-planned process and a reality-based foundation for the actual strategic planning. When you have the results of the research, then you are ready to schedule the strategic planning retreat. Usually an off-site retreat is best for participation, process, and outputs, because people will not be distracted and can focus entirely on the planning activity. Relaxed time together including evenings will produce a better result for both teambuilding and strategic planning.

The following suggestions for a three-day retreat are based on my experience in numerous planning sessions for organizations varying in size, from a dozen staff members up to those with thousands around the world. The first day of the retreat sets the foundation for the planning activity. The second day determines the strategic directions. The third day is dedicated to operational planning and culture. Appendix 3 presents a template three-day agenda for your strategic planning retreat, which also serves as a high-level view of the retreat's structure.

A smaller organization with one or two staff could complete this strategic planning activity in one or two days, and an all-volunteer community organization could do it during several community meetings. Research for these organizations can be simple: ask your board members and volunteers for their thoughts and recommendations, interview a few important stakeholders, survey twenty people in your target market, ask random people you meet about their thoughts, and read widely and listen to what is going on around you. Identify barriers you face, keep your mind open, search for answers, and get others to do the same. Then come together to share what you know and build your plan.

Step 2: Create a common understanding of reality and possibilities for the planning group

The work of the first day of the retreat is to develop a clear understanding of the *realities* facing the organization and to begin to think creatively about future *possibilities*. It is also about getting people to feel comfortable with each other. This is important, because people from different functions will be analyzing and participating in decisions about other departments. Everyone working together is good for the organization! Larger organizations with staff who do not know each other well would benefit from holding a reception the evening before the retreat begins.

The tasks in Day One of the retreat are two-fold:

A. Plans and findings – to set the framework in reality

- Expected results of the retreat
- Review of your organization's history
- Lessons learned from recent evaluations and reports
- Conclusions from competitor and donor assessments
- Survey findings for the various groups of stakeholders
- Current program analysis including results of participant surveys

- Current fundraising analysis including results of donor surveys
- Current financial/administration analysis with results of staff surveys
- Findings and recommendations by the consultant including key points from interviews
- Lessons learned during implementation of the current strategic plan
- A practical, objective, and honest review of the landscape your organization faces

B. Creative steps – to expand your thinking to new heights
- Brainstorming for the dreams and aspirations you have as visionaries
- Identifying the needs and expectations of donors, volunteers, participants, and partners
- Brainstorming desired long-term results you have as mission-driven planners

To achieve meaningful results, make sure you provide the proper physical and emotional environment for interaction, open thinking, discussion, and analysis. It is also important to capture ideas and information during your retreat by having a dedicated notetaker or reporter in each session. I find using PowerPoint slides is the most effective way to record, share, review, and report conclusions as you proceed. When people see what they just agreed, it is easy to confirm or amend.

The inputs from the research findings and creative brainstorming are introductions to the actual drafting of strategic plans. They are open processes designed to create a common body of knowledge and understanding by participants of the real situation in which you are working and to identify potential innovations you might pursue to create breakthroughs in your work. The research reports and creative brainstorming sessions during the retreat both ground and stretch everyone's thinking into new realms and new possibilities!

Taking time to complete the research and address other considerations prior to your retreat will support the creation of a strategic plan that is grounded in reality but also stretching to future possibilities. A strategic plan based on inaccurate or incomplete information will reach wrong conclusions, and a plan built without vision or optimism will achieve little or no success.

Step 3: Draft the key components of the strategic plan

The work of the second day is to draft the big strategic directions in the plan. Based on the research and creativity from the first day, these next steps define the components in the plan that will guide everything you do for the next few years. This includes defining your vision, mission, values, and strategic goals and also key strategies, positioning, credibility, and culture.

By responding to your team's dreams and aspirations and the needs and expectations of your stakeholders, you will develop an effective strategic plan. You specifically need to address the organization's shortcomings candidly to motivate both staff and volunteers and to achieve better results.

The most significant challenge in strategic planning is to base everything on current reality (grounded and realistic) and, at the same time, to be optimistic and stretching (visionary and entrepreneurial) in what you want to achieve.

The tasks in Day Two of the retreat are:

- *Vision:* What you ideally want to see in the world
- *Mission:* What you do to work toward your vision of the ideal world
- *Values:* What you hold most dearly and that guide you in all you do
- *SWOT:* Internal strengths and weaknesses + external opportunities and threats
- *Critical issues:* Key concerns you must address in the three to five years of your plan
- *Strategic goals:* What you must achieve to succeed in three to five years
- *Key strategies:* How you will work
- *Strategic positioning:* Who you are in a competitive marketplace
- *Credibility:* Why people can trust you
- *Organization culture:* The working environment you need to support your goals, strategies, and objectives (larger organizations should defer this topic to later)

At a three-day planning event, I recommend a relaxed dinner at the end of day two. In some cases, you may already have clear and solid statements for some components of your plan. This is often the situation if you are building this year's plan on the basis of a successful strategic plan that was implemented in past years; nevertheless, it is well worth the effort to review these components in light of the research you have just completed.

You may find from your research, as I have on many occasions, that while the program may be good, it is not appealing enough to donors. The challenge is to find ways to make the program strategy even better and also more appealing to donors. This is not being "donor driven" or doing whatever a big donor may want; it is a smart way to find the essential appeal in what you do in your program to attract new donors. As a program worker said to me, "I get it. Fundraising is my job – that's my responsibility and my salary."

In every situation, I have seen that it is productive to review everything with open minds and candid discussions, recognizing that your research has probably revealed new information and your environment has certainly changed. For example, based on your new knowledge, can you find new ways to increase fundraising revenues and develop program plans that appeal to more donors?

As I mentioned earlier in this book, when I was president and national executive director of Foster Parents Plan, we tripled donations from $10 million to $30 million ($64 million in today's value) thanks to more effective marketing and fundraising campaigns and thanks to developing programs with more donor appeal. Our ability to triple donations was a direct result of good strategic planning, excellent staff work, and investment in the fundraising effort.

Step 4: Draft the key components of the operational plans

While the first day of the retreat is focused on setting the foundation for planning and the second day is focused on the strategic level of planning, the third day's focus is on operational planning. Based on the outputs of the first two days (research findings and new strategic directions), you can now draft your operational plans for the organization, departments, teams, and individuals.

These operational plans flow from and implement (that is, operationalize) the strategic plan. The operational plans cascade down in the organization from top management to each department, each team, and every individual. Operational plans define more precisely what people (as departments, teams, and individuals) will do day-to-day to achieve objectives in the current year. Of course, the objectives are all based on research findings, SWOT analysis, donor assessments, creative sessions, strategic goals, and everything else in your new strategic thinking.

Whereas the strategic plan shows the long-term strategic directions to guide what you do, the operational plans show the more immediate objectives and month-to-month activities and deadlines. They present:

- Objectives that are measurable
- Activities that are specific
- Responsibilities, deadlines, and indicators that are clear
- Resources (budget for staff and other expenses) for each department and team
- Supervisory responsibilities to monitor, support, and adapt operational plans as necessary

The time period for the operational plan is your fiscal year or a shorter period up to the end of your current fiscal year. Each major function in the organization such as program, fundraising, and finance/administration has a separate set of operational plans. Larger organizations may have separate departments for media and public relations, advocacy and lobbying, monitoring and evaluation, talent management (human resources), learning and development, and other functions.

The operational plans are best drafted by the people who will actually be responsible for implementing them. This is important, because these staff members and volunteers are the most informed, skilled, and responsible for their particular function. Drafting their own plans leads to better quality and greater commitment to implement their respective plan. In large NGOs with branch offices and numerous staff, representatives of the different work functions should participate in the planning activity.

Managers, of course, provide overall direction and guidance during drafting as well as approval of the plans. Managers also challenge staff to aim higher and stretch, within reason.

The tasks for operational planning in Day Three are:
- Review overall strategic directions from the previous day.
- Brainstorm possible objectives for the year.
- Draft objectives, strategies, activities, and responsibilities for each department.
- Review and comment on the topline department objectives and strategies.
- Present how management will monitor, support, and adjust work during the year.
- Set the framework for a mid-term review to make updates and adjustments.
- Discuss the next steps after the retreat.
- Celebrate a successful retreat!

At the end of the third planning day, you should have a clear idea of the objectives for the organization as a whole and for each major department. In a relatively small organization, you can complete the operational plans in one day or less. In larger organizations, you will not have the complete operational plans, because the staff members who did not attend the strategic planning retreat need to be involved in drafting plans for their level of work. However, the top-level plans for each department should be completed.

It is important to note that your strategic plan and operational plans can be "short and sweet." Depending on the complexity of your nonprofit, you probably do not need extremely lengthy or highly detailed plans. When you keep this critical point in mind, it makes the planning process less daunting and, certainly, more doable.

For community organizations, the operational plans can be quite simple. Such a plan could consist of five to ten objectives and a one-page statement for each objective to be achieved with a brief list of activities to get there, responsibilities, deadlines, indicators of progress, budget, and supervision.

Strategic Planning (3 to 5 Years)

1. Vision	Our ideal world
2. Mission	What we do
3. Core Values	Our fundamental beliefs
4. Stakeholders	Whom we serve
5. Critical Issues	What we must solve
6. Strategic Goals	What we must achieve
7. Strategies	How we move forward
8. Strategic Positioning	What makes us special
9. Credibility	Why we can be trusted
10. Organization Culture	How we behave

Operational Planning (1 Year)

1. Objectives — Exactly where we want to be
2. Activities — What we will do day to day
3. Responsibilities — Who does each activity
4. Deadlines — When it will be completed
5. Indicators — Steps to indicate progress
6. Support/Budget — Resources needed
7. Management — Monitoring and supporting
8. Revenues — Money, time and materials
9. Next Steps — Actions to adjust and improve

Step 5: Review and complete the operational plans

The tasks after the retreat are as important as the conclusions of the retreat itself. It is imperative that you take time to:

- Present the strategic and operational plans to all staff.
- Establish a clear deadline to complete or polish all operational plans.
- Complete other needed plans and add detailed planning by units, teams, and individuals.
- Identify the desired organization culture with all staff involved.
- Review all the detailed plans to assure they are challenging and stretching yet achievable.
- Produce an overall budget of projected revenues and expenditures.

- Present the strategic and operational plans and budget for board approval.
- Celebrate at a staff meeting after final departmental plans are approved.

The first time you prepare a strategic and operational plan is always the most difficult. Each time you do it, it gets easier.

To facilitate the process, plan to use the worksheets included in this book. I have used and refined these worksheets over the past five decades with scores of clients and thousands of NGO executives. In addition, a full set of detailed worksheets and other tools are available at my website: www.NGOFutures.com.

Step 6: Address critical organizational issues

Another level of planning is for organizational development (OD), which deals with more fundamental elements of the organization including its capacity, leadership, and structure. As an organization grows and ages (yes, all organizations age), it will face new issues and new challenges, and you should pay increasing attention to these fundamental OD issues.

Some organizational development issues can be included in the strategic and operational planning. In your operational plans, for example, you should include such issues as the process you use to monitor and evaluate your organization's programs and its fundraising, how you provide staff training and promote learning, how you review staff performance, and how you manage change.

On the other hand, many organizational development issues are extremely high level and highly sensitive; they should be addressed by the board or a special taskforce appointed by the board. These issues include the performance of the executive director, strengthening of the board itself, and overall organizational structure.

Other high-level issues identified in the planning process should be presented separately to the board for approval. Such issues could include the name the organization uses in the marketplace, geographic expansion of the program, other types of expansion, substantial increases in the fundraising and marketing effort, creation of an honorary board, plans to gear up advocacy work, and other significant innovations.

Organizational development issues can include:

- *Leadership:* What is needed to lead the organization to greater achievement?
- *Change issues:* How do you promote and manage the change process?
- *Board of directors:* How does the board move to its next stage of development?
- *Management:* How do you assure managers achieve their objectives?
- *Structure:* How are you structured to achieve your goals?
- *Evaluation:* How do you make monitoring and evaluation strategic?
- *Training:* How do you develop and provide needed training to develop staff talent?
- *Learning:* How does the organization learn? How could it learn better?
- *Knowledge:* How do you retain key lessons? Manage document retention?
- *Workplace:* How do you recruit staff and assure a safe, fair, respectful workplace?
- *Risk management:* How will you avoid or minimize possible risks?

- *Ethics:* What should you do to prevent any potential scandal? How do you respond if there is one?

Caution: Why strategic plans can fail

In my work, I have seen that strategic plans can fail in good organizations. Why? First, at the *strategic planning level*, the major reason for failure is that plans were built on incomplete research into donor, beneficiary, and other stakeholder views and assessments. Other reasons strategic plans fail include:

- Ignoring weaknesses and threats
- Having an uninspiring vision
- Having a long and catch-all mission
- Developing strategies that do not show how to do things

Clear leadership, good planning, and positive culture are the best antidotes to these potential failures.

Second, at the *operational planning level*, failure comes from having incomplete plans or not having measurable objectives, clear responsibilities, and firm deadlines. Also, failure to prioritize and focus on a limited number of key objectives can be a major problem. Another problem is failure to push the planning process to include all units, teams, and individuals. Good management and effective monitoring and evaluation are the best antidotes for these problems.

Third, at the *implementation level*, failure can result from lack of management support, lack of clear delegation, culture conflicts, or lack of adjusting plans as conditions change. The biggest reason for failure is the feeling by staff that the plan was imposed on them – "It's not my plan. If only they had consulted with me!" Participatory planning and progress indicators are the antidote for this.

Finally, at the *organization development level*, failure comes from neglecting to address important but hidden issues. Top staff and board members should be asking, "What are we missing? What might prevent us from achieving great things? What if…?" All of these failures can be avoided if you think strategically.

Catch the wind by creating good strategic and operational plans with an organization culture that unifies everyone in working together to achieve the results you want. Mix realism and optimism to get a stretching but feasible set of objectives.

My work with Romanian NGOs is an example of the success of good research and good planning. A previous program to get thousands of orphans in Romanian institutions placed with families had failed. At the end of that program 20,000 children had been placed with families. Tragically, after a few months most of the children had been returned to institutions, because the foreign donor's funding for their foster parents had discontinued.

I was recruited in the next effort with a similar goal for 20,000 institutionalized children, but this time with a second goal to work through Romanian NGOs that would continue the needed financial support for the children. I provided training and consulting support to twenty-two Romanian NGOs that needed guidance on grant proposals, strategic and operational planning, diversification of fundraising strategies, managing change, and leadership and board development. About 20,000 kids were placed with families with local support systems, and years later most of those NGOs were continuing their work as self-sustaining organizations – raising funds and managing programs for the children. Strengthening local NGOs through strategic planning and support was the successful approach!

Consider "unintended consequences" and "What if?"

In your planning, you will identify what you want to be the consequences of everything you do such as program results, new donors, increased revenues, stronger board, and committed staff. However, there may be consequences you did not anticipate. The classic example is the plan by Mao Zedong to eliminate flies, fleas, rats, and tree sparrows from China, because they were destroying food in granaries. The plan was amazingly successful with everyone catching and killing vast numbers of the vermin and birds. However, sparrows had eaten other pests in large quantities. With sparrows gone, these other pests thrived and destroyed most of the next harvest. The unintended consequence was a failed harvest and starvation! So you do need to think through what might be unintended consequences from your plans.

A useful exercise is to have a session where people ask "What if?" to identify a range of possible unexpected external events, changes in government policy, serious scandal, a shortfall in revenues, and other possible disasters – even big new opportunities. Be sure to ask what if certain bad things happen and also "What if we have extraordinarily good results in program or fundraising? How do we capitalize on success?" Then explore possible solutions or actions for each of the issues identified. These steps are increasingly needed in times of rapid change and uncertainty. No one apparently asked "What if?" in that first program for kids in Romania, and the program collapsed. The NGO participants in the second program often asked that question and then answered it with plans. It is so important to be prepared! Be sure to reward those who are asking questions, even the difficult ones.

Questions for implementation

1. Are you comfortable with the process and flow to create a good strategic plan and operational plans?

2. Have you identified an internal or external consultant with the skills to facilitate the strategic planning process?

3. Do you have the necessary buy-in to hold an off-site, three-day strategic planning retreat or the appropriate process for your smaller NGO? If so, have you identified the participants?

"Let's plan, so we can get organized!
But first, let's get organized, so we can plan!"

3

Preparation and research for strategic and operational planning – Start Now

Now I want you to think strategically about this entire planning process, especially regarding what you expect to accomplish and the timetable to create your organization's new strategic and operational plans. Take time to step through the preparatory process. You must get well organized and lay a solid foundation before you begin to lead the actual process of creating your plans. This chapter gives you all the tools you need for preparation and research. Use the worksheets to complete the research, starting as soon as you are ready.

Step 1: Create the organizing team

The first step is gathering an organizing team to guide the overall process. This small group of individuals should have a strong commitment to the organization's development and represent different parts of the organization. They will not do the actual planning – they just make sure the process is sound.

The organizing team will be responsible for planning all preparations for the retreat, organizing the research to be done, and deciding on the agenda, participants, and schedule. The team should be a manageable size and probably no more than three to five participants. If a particular function in the organization needs strengthening, the director of that function should be included in the team.

Organizational Planning Includes Many Steps
Plan the process
Research the reality
Imagine the possibilities
Determine strategic directions
Plan systems for operations and work
Learn through monitoring and evaluation
Improve individual and team performance
Support through management and governance
Build civil society and a culture of philanthropy

In a large organization, representatives from each department or function should participate. One or two other staff who are good facilitators, strategic thinkers, or emerging leaders could be included. In a community organization, the participants should include the key organizers. In an association or federation, the organizing team should include representatives of member organizations in order to reflect their perspective in the planning process.

The organizing team is also responsible for organizing specific details for the retreat including arranging the facilities and meals, preparing the participants, and assuring conditions for work are optimal during the retreat. The team should review Appendix 1 (What needs to be done in your strategic plan?) and Appendix 2 (Considerations to prepare for your strategic planning) to help determine the process and priorities for the planning.

Here are examples of organizing teams from some of my recent client projects:

- For the West Broadway Neighborhood Association, a neighborhood development organization in Providence, Rhode Island, the organizing team included the executive director, a key volunteer, and myself as the consultant. In a subsequent session, the board chair, another board member, and several volunteers joined us. To lay the foundation for a successful retreat, our organizing team prepared by holding consultations with all board members, key volunteers, and several donors. As consultant, I supported the process with a detailed plan of action for the planning, much like what I am writing here.

- For NYC Kids Project, an artistic education organization that needed to recreate itself as an independent NGO, a meeting of the two founders and myself launched the strategic planning process. The next step was hosting a kickoff party for the founders, some teachers, volunteers, and friends. About fifty people were invited and twenty-five attended. An official representative of the city attended and endorsed the project. Everyone who attended agreed to participate in the next step: planning the project's future. The kickoff party brought together participants for the planning process, which led to a strategic planning day with a dozen participants.

- For a large and well-established community development organization in Colombia, the organizing team started with the fundraising director and myself and, later, the executive director. Thirty people participated in the planning sessions.

- For the Ukrainian Down Syndrome Organization, the strategic planning activity was initiated during one of my meetings with the fundraising director, which led to further involvement of the board chair. This was the organizing team. Other board members and staff made up the planning group.

In each case, the small organizing team met to establish the process and clarify the next steps. When you establish the organizing team, it's important to communicate to other staff what you are doing and the reasons why.

Step 2: Determine the planning method, facilitation process, and consulting support

After you have convened the organizing team, ask the team members to address these questions:

- Why is planning needed now?
- What do we want to see as the output of the planning process?
- Who should be involved in the planning sessions?
- What information do we have now that should be considered? Who will prepare this?
- What new information do we need? How will we get this? Who will get it?
- Where will the planning sessions take place? Who is responsible for arrangements?
- How do we assure we have a good approach and tools for the sessions?
- Who will guide the process? Who will facilitate? Who will report?
- How do we assure everyone will support the plans?
- How do we assure the plans will be approved when completed?

- How do we assure the plans will be implemented?
- What else should we be asking?

Next, be sure to plan a good facilitation process. It is critically important that all voices are heard and all participants are able to speak candidly. In collecting feedback from groups, for example, it is efficient to have each group take turns reporting just one key conclusion rather than having the first group's report cover every aspect, thereby leaving less for other groups to share. Skill and experience are needed to facilitate large meetings as well as small group work to elicit honest feedback, move discussions forward, synthesize information, and keep everyone interested and involved.

A skilled facilitator makes all this possible. As mentioned earlier, an impartial and respected staff member or a volunteer with organizational development skills could be given this responsibility. You can also recruit an experienced external consultant.

The consultant works with the organizing team to organize the planning process, review key documents, assure a clear grasp of issues facing the organization, and ensure a smooth and productive process. As a reminder, I use the term consultant to refer to the person with this responsibility, whether she or he is recruited internally or externally.

If you choose to hire a professional consultant, remember to negotiate an appropriate level of compensation for consulting services. My approach is to find a level that is within the organization's budgetary ability and is fair to both the organization and the consultant.

Step 3: Establish the information management process

You should plan how you will capture inputs (reports, summaries, group work, and discussions) and outputs (conclusions about the key elements of the plans) for later use. I have seen organizations record the sessions and then, later, have someone listen to everything and try to extract the outcomes. This is a daunting task! Other organizations ask someone to write down everything they hear or transcribe everything on flip charts after the retreat.

After decades of facilitating planning sessions, I believe the best approach includes these four steps:

A. *For inputs:* Have all summaries and research reports presented concisely in written form, either a Word or PowerPoint document. These can later be appended to the final plan for reference.

B. *For group work:* Have each group select a reporter who will capture the conclusions and recommendations of the group to report back to the larger group in a Word or PowerPoint document.

C. *For conclusions:* Use PowerPoint with a projection system to capture and present the actual wording of key parts of the strategic plan and the objectives of operational plans. Seeing the projected wording of a key section of the plan clarifies thinking, facilitates discussion and rewording, and enables agreement.

D. *For the final plan:* Capture and compile the materials from the first three steps and, by the end of the session, you will have a written version of your strategic plan and topline operational plan.

Step 4: Identify the strategic planning group – those who will participate in the planning retreat

The members of the strategic planning group (also called the strategic planning taskforce or just planning group) are the people who will discuss and actually draft the initial strategic plan during the strategic planning retreat. How you select these participants depends on your history, size, structure, and other factors. The executive director, top managers, and staff representatives should be included. Team leaders, strategic thinkers, good facilitators, experienced researchers, and emerging leaders make excellent participants. Select board members, engaged volunteers, and representatives of program beneficiaries and partners could be included.

A group of ten to twenty-five people is a good size for a strategic planning group for a three-day planning retreat. I find that planning groups of up to fifty participants can be managed, but this larger number of participants makes it necessary to split the group frequently into smaller working groups with a facilitator for each working group, and then reporting and finding consensus in the full group. For larger organizations, you may need to organize separate sessions ahead of time to secure staff input on topics such as situation assessment, their dreams, possible long-term results, donor needs and expectations, potential objectives for each unit, and the desired organization culture.

In a community organization, the strategic planning group should include the organizers, dedicated volunteers, and others who are interested and bring useful views to the planning sessions. In an association or federation, it should include as many representatives of member organizations as possible.

Participation at all levels is important to get the best ideas and gain buy-in and, ultimately, assure successful implementation of the strategic plan.

Step 5: Conduct research and analysis to build the strategic plan on external and internal realities plus imagination and creativity

Research and analysis are necessary inputs to any good planning. So are your dreams and aspirations! There are four requirements here to get the outcomes you want:

- To know how to go forward, you have to know where you have been. This requires *internal research.*
- To know where you want to go, you need to know what is around you. This requires *external research.*
- To expand your horizons, you must use your dreams and your imagination. This requires *visionary thinking.*
- To achieve great success, you aim high and creatively but based on reality. This requires *realistic thinking.*

I have seen plans fail when they are built with insufficient regard for the organization's history, its weaknesses, and external conditions. Careful research and analysis are the only way to avoid the pitfall of mistaken assumptions. The organizing team takes responsibility to assure the needed research and analysis are completed. This team also arranges ways to spur creative and aspirational thinking to bring forth the highest hopes of all participants to guide the planning.

The strategic planning process requires "eyes wide open." This means you have full awareness of your organization without distortion (or denial). You will gain this objective awareness by completing the following research tasks prior to the strategic planning itself. This sequence follows a logical flow, which I have used hundreds of times:

A. Review of the organization's history to establish a common baseline for discussion, prepared by the executive director

B. Lessons learned from past evaluations and reports, prepared by the responsible managers of the relevant units on key lessons to be used in planning and implementation

C. Surveys of program participants, donors, staff, and other stakeholders to learn their views, organized by a designated staff member with guidance by the consultant

D. Competitor assessments to learn what you need to know about them, prepared by selected staff with guidance by the consultant (this can also include partners)

E. Donor assessments conducted by fundraisers to get a sense of where and how to grow income

F. Program analysis including survey results to provide guidance on challenges and opportunities in the nonprofit organization's program, prepared by the program manager

G. Fundraising analysis including survey results to provide guidance on challenges and opportunities in fundraising, prepared by the fundraising manager

H. Finance analysis including survey results to provide guidance on challenges and opportunities in finance/administration, prepared by the finance/administration manager

I. Confidential interviews with key stakeholders to obtain candid input, conducted by the consultant on a confidential basis to assure valid findings

J. An overall report on findings and recommendations, prepared by the consultant based on all the inputs including the confidential interviews

K. Review of the current strategic plan to assess what worked and what did not, prepared by selected staff or the consultant

L. View of the landscape you will encounter presented at the planning session by external experts or board members on important developments and emerging trends

---

It is important to conduct both internal research and external research before you begin the planning *to know your realities, obtain an objective perspective, and gain insights into what your organization can do better. Use the worksheets in this chapter to guide the research.*

The following sections describe each of the research tasks in greater detail. In every case, the report should include the factual research findings, analytical conclusions, and brief recommendations. These steps will produce a strong and realistic introduction as well as a baseline for the actual planning sessions during the strategic planning retreat. You can start now.

Internal research: Review your history

To bring everyone up to date and to establish a common baseline for discussion, it is important to prepare a brief review of your history and your motivation to call people together. This could be a one-page or two-page handout, a flip chart with key points, or a discussion of where you have been and what brought you together. Often, this review is simply a brief account of what has happened recently including major challenges to point everyone in the same general direction.

If someone presents your history orally, it is useful to capture the key points, so you have it for future reference as a reminder to everyone and as an introduction to any newcomers to the process. Perhaps even capture this historical review in a video for later use!

This chapter includes several worksheets. Note that "R" stands for research-related worksheets and "P" stands for planning-related worksheets.

R1 WORKSHEET: HISTORICAL REVIEW

Historical review – The view from the executive director's office (or fundraiser's office)

Note: One page maximum

1. Our founding principles
2. What we most value
3. Our past accomplishments
4. Why we are here
5. Our big challenges

Internal research: Identify lessons learned by reviewing all recent reports and evaluations

Most organizations have numerous reports and evaluations. In fact, most government and foundation grants usually include requirements for an evaluation and report at the end of the grant, and organizations routinely provide progress reports to other donors. As preparation for strategic planning, you should assemble all such reports and evaluations that have been done over the past three to five years.

I recommend assigning several staff members with the task of reviewing the reports and evaluations and then preparing a brief summary of key successes, major obstacles encountered, and lessons learned. Any important internal assessments conducted in the last few years should be included as well.

R2 WORKSHEET: LESSONS LEARNED –
Summary of findings

Lessons learned from the evaluation of XYZ Project –
prepared by (name) and (date)

Note: One page maximum for each report

Our XYZ Project was funded by ABC and operated during
this timeframe:

The objectives were:

The results were:

Total funding was:

Key conclusions are:

1. What we did well
2. What we need to improve
3. Other observations for consideration

Use the Lessons Learned worksheet and make sure summaries are short and candid: just one page for a major report or evaluation, with key points and lessons learned in simple bullet format. Honest analysis will help make sure organizational strengths and successes are reinforced and organizational weaknesses and failures are identified, so they can be addressed and corrected. A collection of these summaries can be distributed before the strategic planning retreat. During the retreat, the individuals who prepared the summaries can present highlights of lessons learned in rapid-fire presentations.

External research: Survey donors, staff, beneficiaries, and other stakeholders

It is essential to obtain the input of your key stakeholders, doing it in a way that guarantees you are getting their honest feedback. Keep in mind that stakeholders are any groups, entities, or individuals that are important for your success. The term *stakeholders* for an NGO is derived from the term *stockholders* for a corporation. Stakeholders include board members, staff, major donors, regular donors, essential volunteers, partners, authorities, program beneficiaries or their representatives, and others who contribute to your success.

The main reason to survey current and potential stakeholders is to learn more about your organization from *their perspective*, so the strategic plan will be based on reality. Findings from such surveys often challenge assumptions and lead to new insights. In addition, conducting surveys lets respondents know you care about their opinion. Plus, this encourages their further involvement and support! Feedback from donors and potential donors may be especially important as this represents expansion or growth opportunities.

Program beneficiaries or participants are those individuals, groups, or society in general that benefit from your programs. They are the most important stakeholders. Some NGOs involve their beneficiaries as participants in the program, other NGOs help beneficiaries who cannot be participants, and some NGOs help society in general. In these last two situations, find representatives or spokespersons for these groups. Feedback from program participants with their views on your program process and results is especially important, since it can validate the program strategy and may lead to significant improvements.

You can survey specific audiences such as:
- Program participants or their representatives
- Current donors
- Former donors
- Potential donors
- Volunteers
- Partners
- Staff members
- Board members
- Government authorities
- The general public

Surveys can be conducted through easy-to-use Internet-based survey tools such as www.SurveyMonkey.com. Many survey formats are also available online along with guidance on constructing effective surveys. A short introductory message and the link to the survey instrument will get you survey results in a few days or a few weeks. Each survey should be adapted for each category of potential respondents, with an appropriate introduction and relevant questions. Make surveys short and easy to complete.

The survey should use multiple-choice questions about views, concerns, and expectations. I recommend including only one or two essay questions for recommendations and general comments. This helps to ensure your survey process is useful and doesn't become burdensome. You don't want the process of reviewing and compiling results to get pushed to the backburner. Staff surveys, volunteer surveys, and donor surveys are the easiest to conduct, because you already have their contact information, and they are accustomed to receiving email from you.

Surveys of donors should include questions about their satisfaction with the organization's activities, reports, communications, and service and what they expect from you. Surveys of staff and volunteers should include questions on internal efficiency and effectiveness, the organization's culture, satisfaction in the workplace, and recommendations for improvements. Surveys of program participants should include questions about program implementation and effectiveness over the long term. Surveys of authorities should include questions about overall benefits to society.

Each group survey should be summarized in a report with answers to the multiple-choice questions, summarized responses to essay questions, and data about the respondents. These survey reports offer critical insight for the strategic planning process.

R3 WORKSHEET: STAKEHOLDER SURVEYS
– Summary of findings

Stakeholder group: _____

– prepared by (name) and (date)

Note: One page maximum for each survey

1. How this stakeholder group helps us
2. What they like most about us
3. In what ways do we disappoint them
4. What we should do better for them
5. Other observations for consideration

If you are a leader or volunteer in a community organization, you can use a handout questionnaire to survey people who are not involved in your organization. Questionnaires help you obtain valuable information and new contacts, plus, you can engage volunteers in the process.

For example, two volunteers of our local environmental organization collected nearly a hundred surveys in just two hours from people at a neighborhood farmers market. To capture their interest, we began these surveys with a few general questions on one particular "green" issue – the theme of the week such as trees, gardens, recycling, water, energy, or transportation. Then we moved on to questions about what they would like to see done for that particular topic and how they could help as volunteers to support the issue. Of course, the volunteers collected people's names and contact information and followed up to encourage volunteerism.

In my work with another neighborhood association, the most important survey results were from members of the community who were not currently involved. We were trying to change the image of the association and recruit more members and volunteers. We asked questions about the most important issues in the community and how the respondent could help to improve the neighborhood. These surveys provided valuable insights to develop and expand the association as well as develop better plans and stronger appeals.

We found that asking people their opinion also got more people to attend monthly meetings and participate in the activities. We also learned that it saved time if we could get people to respond online, so we used portable devices to take the surveys as we walked around the neighborhood. (See Sample Survey.)

SAMPLE SURVEY – Involvement issues

Use this survey for people not currently involved.
(Collect at events and in stores.)

Our community organization wants your opinion on these important issues. Thank you!

1. Do you know about our group? Yes__, No__
2. What do you think of our work? Excellent__, Good__, Fair__, Poor__, Don't Know__
3. What are the big problems in our community? City services__, Education__, Fresh food__, Graffiti__, Green issues__, Housing__, Jobs__, Safety/crime__, Transportation__, Other_____
4. What should we focus on? Arts and culture__, Clean-up activities__, Restaurants__, Crime and safety __, Parks__, Trees__, Transportation__, Education__, Energy __, Community gardens__, Events__, Business__, Sustainable development__, Activities for kids__, Make it the best place to live__
5. What are your dreams for the future of our community?
6. How can our group better serve the community?
7. Would you be willing to help us work on any of the issues you listed? Yes__, No__
8. Would you help? Advocacy__, Events__, Fundraising__, PR__, Office __ Translation___
9. Can we add you to our mailing list for updates about issues and events? Yes__, No___

Name: _____

Address: _____

Email: _____

External research: Analyze competitors and partners to learn from them and to know what you need to do

Many people like to think nonprofits do not compete with each other. The reality, however, is that all nonprofits are in competition with each other to attract attention, funding, volunteers, and other resources. Donors and grant makers can give their support to you or to other nonprofits. Why yours? You need to know how to stand out and be more appealing than other organizations. Donors and other stakeholders want to see a "value added" from your use of their funds. You need to provide it!

What can you learn from your competitors and partners? In addition to understanding how to position yourself in comparison with them, you can learn much from nonprofit competitors, because they have experience in the same work you do. You can learn best practices, successful strategies, and innovative approaches for person-to-person fundraising and mass-media marketing, volunteer and board development, and internal systems and techniques as well as insights from their successes and failures. In addition to learning from competitors, organizations often align as partners with these very same competitors on important public relations, lobbying, and development issues of common interest.

R4 WORKSHEET: COMPETITOR RESEARCH – Short format

ZXCZXC NGO, one of our closest competitors

– prepared by (name) and (date)

Note: One page maximum for each report

Total income for this NGO

1. What we can learn from this NGO
2. What we should avoid that they do
3. How we can differentiate our NGO from them
4. Strategies they use that we should consider
5. Other observations for consideration

External research: Assess representative current donor groups to provide a baseline for the planning

Just as it is important to understand your competitors, you must also understand your donors. This exercise is done by those most familiar with your current donors. It is a preliminary process to make sure you can later share your knowledge and insights based on your personal work with donors. It supplements any surveys you have done.

R5 WORKSHEET FOR CURRENT DONOR ASSESSMENTS – Short format

The fundraising team's assessment of current donor groups
– prepared by (name) and (date)

Note: One page maximum for this report

1. Who are our current donor groups and what do we want from them?
2. What do they want from us?
3. What do we do well?
4. What can we do better?

Internal research: Review realities in program, fundraising, and finance/administration

These three separate, internal reports should be prepared by the directors of program, fundraising, and finance/administration regarding their respective area of responsibility. If your organization has other departments and functions – such as volunteer management, monitoring and evaluation, or education and advocacy – those directors should prepare reports as well. Insights from recent surveys should be included.

The main purpose of these reports is to enable the director of each department to share his or her views on important issues and concerns and to provide a common understanding of the challenges and opportunities in each functional area for all participants in their planning.

R6 WORKSHEET FOR ANALYSIS BY DEPARTMENT DIRECTORS

Director's report on _____ functional area (program, fundraising, finance and administration, or other function)

Note: One page maximum for each report, including survey results

1. What were our achievements and why?
2. What were our shortfalls and why?
3. What did we miss in the process?
4. How can we do better?

External research: Hold confidential interviews with key stakeholders

When I am a consultant for an organization's strategic planning process, one of my most important tasks is to conduct interviews with ten to fifteen of the most important stakeholders (sometimes more depending on the complexity of the issues facing the organization). I prefer to do interviews in person when feasible or by telephone or virtually. The client and I select the people to be interviewed. The client schedules my discussions with the stakeholders, indicating that we are arranging interviews to get confidential feedback as input for the organization's strategic planning process and that no preparation is needed. My interviews usually last thirty to forty-five minutes or, in some cases, an hour.

I always open an interview with the confirmation that everything they say is confidential and that I will take notes and may use some quotations in my report, but that no quotations would be attributed. People tell me that I have a way of making them feel comfortable in being truthful, as I stress we must have their honest input in order to build a strong plan. It is so important to get honest feedback that I repeat several times during an interview that everything I hear will remain confidential and that, for the good of the organization, I need to hear what really needs to be done to strengthen and expand the organization. I say that short answers are best but give lots of encouragement to "Say more about that" on particular topics.

Prior to the discussions with stakeholders, I share with the client a draft of the questions I plan to use including any controversial ones to assure there will be no surprises. (I learned this from the chairman of my board in one organization who made it clear to me that he wanted "no surprises" and that I should share bad news as well as good news with him first.)

I do not provide the interviewees with the questions ahead of time, because I don't want people to think too much about the issues until we talk. A natural flow of conversation is the best way to get insight into the realities of the organization, and I pursue topics by asking about weaknesses or problems to be addressed. One of the most important questions is the last question I always ask: "What else should I have asked you?" This open-ended question often brings out revealing concerns or suggestions that we had not discussed.

Here's a great place to start: Refer to the list of sample questions for key stakeholders, which I most recently used for a large, global NGO. Of course, you should tailor your survey questions to your own organization and the specific stakeholder you are interviewing (for example, a major donor, board member, partner, and so forth).

Sample questions for key stakeholders

Note: Introduce yourself. Begin by thanking the person and confirming confidentiality.

1. How long have you known organization XYZ?
   In what capacity?

2. In your opinion, what does it do best? Please be candid.
   What are its current strengths?

3. How is it unique? Why should it expand its activities?

4. What has it not done well or not done at all?
   Please be candid so weaknesses are addressed.

5. Why do you think it has not already made needed changes?

6. What is its vision? What is the best way to reach this vision?

7. Do you recommend any new goals? New strategies?
   What else?

8. What are its funding needs? Why?

9. What barriers might exist to expand its activities? Increasing its funding? Tell me more.

10. How does it relate to other organizations? Governments?
    Companies? Donors? Participants?

11. What are its organizational needs? Competencies it lacks? Can you give some examples?

12. What structural changes do you recommend? Changes in staff? Changes in the board? Why?

13. What barriers might exist to the changes you recommend? Can you tell me more?

14. What are your highest hopes for the organization and what it might achieve?

15. What else should I have asked you? What concerns have we not covered?

The sample questions may seem to be imposing or intrusive, but without learning what stakeholders really believe, you cannot clearly see the issues and understand exactly what to address.

Conducting confidential interviews with key stakeholders is one of the most delicate - and most important - steps in the strategic planning process. Confidentiality is essential.

Confidential interviews are best conducted by someone who is not involved in the organization. Keep in mind that donors, staff, board members, and others are more likely to give honest opinions to someone they fully trust.

If you do these interviews yourself (very difficult to do) or through an internal consultant, you need to remember that it is challenging to get stakeholders to be honest during a personal interview conducted by someone involved in the organization. Whoever conducts the interviews should confirm the confidentiality of the discussion and repeat several times, "I do want your honest assessment and response to this question. We need to know about any concerns you have. Your comments are confidential."

What is the output of these interviews? It is a confidential report on findings and recommendations. (My reports vary from three to ten pages, depending on the complexity of the organization and its challenges.) The report's findings and recommendations should be honest reflections of key points in the interviews. It is a good idea to include a selection of representative quotes presenting praise and suggestions for change (unattributed, of course).

To follow a practice of "no surprises," the organization's leadership team will want to read this confidential report prior to the strategic planning sessions. The findings and recommendations from key stakeholders will help to ensure the strategic plan will be based on reality and reflect what stakeholders really think. (In the strategic planning retreat, I usually present a findings and recommendations report after the other research has been presented.)

R7 WORKSHEET: LESSONS FROM CONFIDENTIAL INTERVIEWS

Lessons from interviews with key stakeholders

1. What were our organization's main achievements and why?
2. What were our main shortfalls and why?
3. What new strategies should we consider?
4. What are the main internal issues?
5. What are other changes we should consider?
6. Other issues?

Internal research: Review your previous or current strategic plan

Preparation for the strategic planning retreat should include an assessment of your last strategic plan including the process used to draft the plan, its implementation, and its results (an objective assessment of hits and misses). The organizing team should assess and report on this, or ask the consultant to do this. The goal is to determine what you should continue doing and what you should do differently to create your new strategic plan. It is very important to improve the planning process each time around. You can use the worksheet below to review your previous or current strategic plan.

R8 WORKSHEET: LESSONS FROM OUR CURRENT STRATEGIC PLAN

Lessons about our last strategic planning process and implementation

Note: One page maximum

1. How did the planning process work?
2. What were our achievements and why?
3. What were our shortfalls and why?
4. What did we miss in the process?
5. How can we do better this time around?

External research: Sharing is learning!

When I was working at Save the Children in the United States, I took the unusual step of convening a meeting of fundraising directors from our five major competitors. We met frequently over the years, and we learned to share with each other. During successive meetings over the next few years, we all learned amazing things about how the others were operating. This was the best learning possible, because we were competing in the same field, and we had very similar products to offer. We shared and we all got better! In fact, each organization's fundraising results and program impacts increased significantly year after year.

I am revisiting the issue of competitor research here, because it is such an important learning step. To do competitor research, I suggest you first list the five to seven organizations that are doing the most similar or comparable work to your own. Then assign one or two of these organizations to a likely member of the planning group to conduct research and come back with a report and recommendations. Completing this task should take less than a day or two.

Start by visiting the organization's website and looking for key documents such as "About Us" and their annual reports, plans, board members, financials, and how they work. You can call the organization and ask about their successes, how they operate, how they implement programs, and how they treat donors. Meet with them if you can – it is amazing how much organizations are willing to share or brag about or complain about. Ask others what they know about that organization and what they think about it.

In one organization, a member of the staff became a regular donor to its five closest competitors. She could accurately track how quickly they responded, what they said, how they treated donors, and how they responded to questions about program results, overhead figures, plans for growth, and so forth. While you could conduct this competitive research as a "secret shopper," I recommend being open and honest with everyone as you conduct your investigation.

The net result of this research is a two-page report on how each of your close competitors works and, specifically, what you might learn from them either by copying their efforts or by jumping ahead of them. You can more clearly understand your unique added value and how to differentiate yourself from your closest competitors. You may identify issues of common interest where you might join together for more effective advocacy or lobbying. These reports are shared early in the planning process, so your planning group gets a better sense of the world around you.

R9 WORKSHEET: COMPETITOR RESEARCH – Long format

Note: Two pages maximum for each organization

1. Name of organization and contact information
2. The vision, mission, and core values statement
3. Services offered and population served
4. Fundraising, financial, and staffing information
5. Strengths – What can we learn from them?
6. Weaknesses – What should we avoid and where can we excel?
7. Uniqueness – How can we stand out?
8. Possibilities for cooperation
9. Recommendations for setting new benchmarks for our organization

---

With these research findings, you will be prepared to provide everyone with a good grounding in reality for the strategic planning retreat. In Part II, we move on to explore what you need to know about values and culture – how to assess your current values and culture and make sure you have strong core values and the new, desired culture you need, which you will discuss on the third day of the strategic planning retreat.

R10 WORKSHEET: PREPARATION FOR THE PLANNING

1. Issues to be addressed:
2. Board support confirmed:
3. Organizing team members:
4. Facilitation and reporting assignments:
5. Participants in the planning sessions:
6. Research completed:
7. Dates, locations, and details for the sessions:
8. Agenda prepared:
9. Processes confirmed:
10. Worksheets downloaded:
11. Other issues:

Questions for implementation

1. Are you ready to establish the organizing team and give them precise instructions? (Refer to the list of questions in this chapter.)

2. Are you ready to establish the information management process so all reports, discussion summaries, and conclusions will be captured and shared throughout the planning process?

3. The worksheets for research in this chapter are easy to use. Have you asked selected staff to conduct and complete the research before the planning sessions?

4. Now is the time to launch the research work. When will you have completed all worksheets in this chapter?

You can reach out to stakeholders through virtual media.
They want to hear from you.

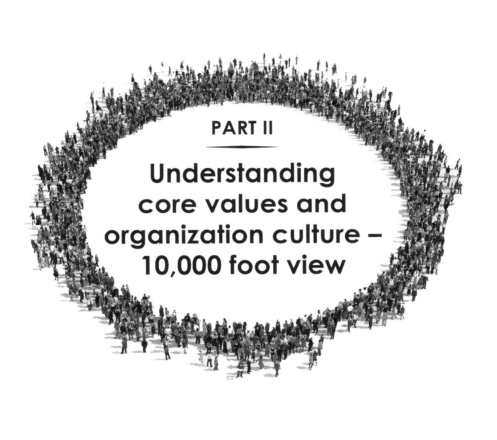

PART II

Understanding
core values and
organization culture –
10,000 foot view

W hich statement best describes your organization?

- Culture at organization A: Passion for the mission, obsession with growth, commitment to customer service, and "let everyone shine"
- Culture at organization B: Donor-run, inward looking, committed, hardworking, blaming, firefighting, dysfunctional

In this section we look at beliefs and behaviors, since it is important to assure that everyone actually works together to support the strategic plan and operational plans. Keep in mind that organizational success depends on these five essentials for nonprofit organizations:

1. The organization's perceived value to society
2. Its effectiveness in delivering results
3. Its efficiency in administration
4. Its trustworthiness in everything it does and says
5. Its transparency to donors and other stakeholders

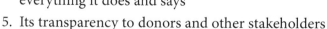

Your core values and organization culture serve to guide everyone's approach to all these essential components for your organization.

Organizations often wonder why their strategic plans fall short of expectations. Such failures may be caused by a conflict in values or an organization culture that does not support your strategic plan. At your organization, you can have a culture that either supports or undercuts your leadership and your planning.

In this part of the book, I will lead you through the process of understanding the core values and organization culture you need to achieve success in your strategic plan and operational plans. Whether you acknowledge it or not, values and culture operate in every organization, and they greatly influence behavior and results. In any event, it is up to you to address the situation. Values and culture are key components of leading and managing that are too frequently neglected in an organization, but they have always received priority attention from me as a fundraiser, executive, and consultant.

Here, you will learn the importance of core values and organization culture, understand their influence on people's effectiveness and efficiency, and know the steps to assure they support your operations. Along the way, you will work with proven tools related to values and culture.

Whether you are the executive director, fundraiser, or other staff member who cares about results, you can initiate and lead an effort to revise or update the organization's values and culture, so they support fundraising, program, and everything else you do. In too many organizations, I have seen that failure to get culture right has been neglected. I have also seen the initiative to get it right come from people who held various roles in organizations: an executive director, a board member, or a young staff member. It is too important to neglect.

According to Alan Murry, editor of *Fortune*, "Leadership is crucial to culture, but fixing a broken one is no easy task." Culture is broken in many organizations. It takes conscious attention and concerted effort to get it right.

The next three chapters build on smart leadership, strategic plans, and meaningful teamwork to ensure you have the strong core values and organization culture you need. The objective of working on both values and culture is to enable you to lead others in the organization to:

1. Understand the components and significance of core values and organization culture.
2. See how getting values and culture right is a necessary strategy for success.
3. Work with proven tools to identify or confirm strong values and design the needed culture.
4. Master the steps to overcome barriers and reinforce strong values and your new, desired culture.

The next three chapters cover what you must understand before you get to working on values and culture – and to get others to start thinking about the need for strong values and the right culture for growth and development.

4

Core values as non-negotiable beliefs and the foundation of everything

Core values are the non-negotiable beliefs that underlie and guide an organization internally as well as communicating something important to external stakeholders. They are the foundation of an organization. As a young executive director said to me, "Core values are like the programming in our minds of what is right and what is wrong." A conflict in values within an organization is the most difficult conflict to resolve, because values are so fundamental and non-negotiable in determining behavior. Conflict based on different values or beliefs has led to many (if not most) confrontations within a society as well as wars between societies.

Core values are the fundamental beliefs of a group. Core values are the basis of culture. Your values are what make you trustworthy.

Along with its vision and mission, an organization's core values are the most important components of strategic planning and should form a mutually reinforcing statement about the organization, why it exists, what it does, and why it can be trusted.

Your planning group can gain important insights by discussing the relative significance of vision, mission, and values. Which is most important for your organization? Which is most important to your stakeholders? How does any one of these three – vision, mission, or values – help determine the others? Do they form a solid base for all you do?

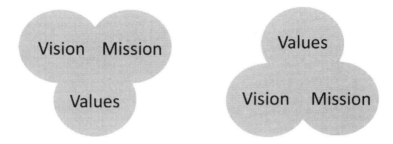

What is the relative significance of Vision and Mission and Values?

Taken together, your organization's vision, mission, and values should have strong appeal to attract people to join you in pursuit of a better world. When you have clear and powerful statements of these three components, people will want to be involved with you. This includes staff, board members, donors, volunteers, partners, and even program participants or beneficiaries. These three statements are essential when communicating to current and potential stakeholders.

Core values are what you hold and value most of all. As the most fundamental beliefs, principles, or norms, they shape how an organization pursues its vision and carries out its mission. They influence activities in the organization as well as relationships with outside groups. Core values guide everything you do and say. Values are enduring and non-negotiable. They are the basis of an organization's culture; they strengthen program, advocacy, and public education.

Some core values such as honesty, hard work, or making a difference may be the same in many nonprofits. Other core values will vary significantly from organization to organization. For example, an environmental organization, a child-protection organization, and a human-rights organization may all hold integrity and hard work as core values, but they will have different values appropriate to their vision and mission such as the value, respectively, of science, compassion, and the law. An organization's values may include belief in the dignity of poor people, education as the pathway to progress, kindness to animals, spiritual convictions, or any other belief that is cherished and held in high esteem. The values that are essential for an organization – and guide its vision, mission, culture, fundraising, and program – should be articulated in its values statement.

It is important to confirm, clarify, update, or identify your organization's core values – and make sure they are strong values.

Your nonprofit's values may need to be confirmed or clarified or, in some cases, updated. Here is a preview of how to address an organization's values:

1. A process of *values confirmation* is worthwhile even if your organization already has a clear statement of its values. Many organizations were born from the values of the founders or have had a long-standing statement of values. These organizations would benefit from reviewing these traditional values to reaffirm them, assure they are currently valid, and ensure new employees, board members, and volunteers know the values they are expected to follow. Later in this chapter, I discuss the idea of identifying *strong* core values, which rise

above the typical values statement. With this in mind, I encourage all nonprofits to not simply confirm their values, but clarify, update, or identify their strong core values.

2. *Values clarification* would be appropriate to explore your organization's current values statement, discuss why you believe in these particular values, and what that implies. This may be especially important early in a strategic planning process and for new employees to assure their agreement and support.

3. A *values update* may be appropriate in the wake of current economic and social changes. If external conditions have changed significantly for your organization or you are considering substantial changes in your vision and mission statements, the values statement you have followed in the past should be reexamined and updated.

4. *Values identification* is essential if your organization does not have a clear written statement of its core values. An organization's leaders may assume there are generally agreed values, but if they are not identified and agreed in a values statement, there could be contrary views among staff. This could result in confusion and internal conflict.

Statements of core values

Values statements can vary widely and, as noted above, directly reflect core beliefs that are specific to each organization. The examples in the box illustrate how different organizations define their core values.

Values of a youth NGO	Values of a faith-based NGO	Values of an education NGO
1. Activating leadership 2. Demonstrating integrity 3. Living diversity 4. Enjoying participation 5. Striving for excellence 6. Acting sustainably	1. The intrinsic value created in the image and likeness of God 2. Christian principles of stewardship, love, compassion, interdependence, and identity 3. Dignity, integrity, and freedom 4. That people matter	1. Caring for children 2. Networking with others 3. Celebrating success 4. Respecting others 5. Striving for high quality 6. Welcoming innovations 7. Sharing with others

The values of these three organizations illustrate how values are, in fact, part of your program delivery. As I was working with all three nonprofits, I saw values as the basis of who they are, how they behave, what they say, and what they do. I saw that they actually built their programs and their fundraising on their strong core values.

Values statements can be short or a little longer, but they must get to the essence of what is fundamental to the organization. I personally prefer short statements, because short is memorable. This helps ensure your stakeholders can readily recall (and live by) your organization's shared values. Although some values in the examples may appear to be objectives or behaviors, the determining concept is that the organization's leaders, staff, and board members hold them as core values to guide them in what they do. Only the organization itself can articulate what it believes! What you believe is what you include.

Although core values are the non-negotiable beliefs and foundation of everything in your organization, they do need to be reviewed in a strategic planning exercise to assure they are up to date and precisely what you want. Whether you decide to confirm, clarify, update, or identify your nonprofit's core values, you and your team can follow the steps below. This is a preview of what you will do in the planning session.

Preview: Step-by-step guidance to confirm, clarify, update, or identify your values statement

When you get to the planning itself, I encourage you to download my planning tool – "Assessing Our Core Values and Culture" – from my website (www.NGOFutures.com) to support this process. The objective is to produce a clear and short values statement that is motivating and guiding for current and prospective employees, volunteers, and other stakeholders! I find the following process is most successful.

First, the leader of the organization shares his or her views on what the fundamental values are and asks for candid and honest participation. In fact, in the opening discussion of core values, you might ask several people to tell a story that illustrates what they think the organization holds as its most deeply felt values.

Then, follow these three steps:

1. Identify the big changes in the world and for your work in the coming planning period. These changes will have significant impact on everyone's daily responsibilities and should guide your thinking in these steps. Think individually and then discuss in small groups to get your group's consensus on the big changes in the world and in your work. Write the group statement as "big changes in world and work." The groups present their conclusions to the full meeting, and you develop a consensus on what these big changes are for both world and work.

2. Identify what you believe are the current core values of the organization. Here it is especially important to work individually and then in small groups. To get full involvement and commitment, each person identifies what he or she thinks are the organization's current core values, then each small group has an open and candid discussion to identify a consensus on core values. The groups present their conclusions and, together, everyone works to gain consensus on what the organization's current core values really are.

3. The next work is to identify changes that should be made in your values statement based on what you have identified as big changes above. Use the same sequence of individual work, small group work, and full group work to move toward full consensus. My planning tool, "Assessing Our Core Values and Culture," will assist you in this process.

Here is one way the group process can optimize participation and get a good result:

1. Ask a facilitator to lead the process.
2. Ask everyone to keep their comments short, so everyone has time to participate.
3. Ask everyone to share what they think is the most important value first.
4. Go around the group to hear one comment per person rather than one person reciting a list.
5. Ask everyone in the group to listen to what others have to say and consider their views.
6. Keep the list on a flip chart or PowerPoint slide that everyone in the group can see.

7. As you move from person to person, ask everyone to agree or add to what is already on the list.

8. Ask anyone who shares a new value to articulate briefly the reason it should be added.

9. Find a way to combine similar values or build them into something bigger.

10. Identify the five or six important values that reflect consensus.

11. Compare this values statement with your vision and mission to confirm a good fit.

The values statement is respected and revered as the foundation of the organization. The values are included in your strategic plan and reflected in operational plans, proposals, communications, posters, and fundraising and program documents. The values are accepted as essential to the organization's being, behavior, and work.

Let your *strong* core values activate your program

Sonia Velazquez, executive director of Literature for All of Us, a dynamic youth organization in Chicago, believes we need strong values today. Sonia previously served as executive director of an NGO combatting child labor in international corporations and served as CEO of a private foundation focused on human rights work. She believes: "Given the reality we are living right now and how the world has been changed by the COVID-19 pandemic and the Black Lives Matter movement, the component of values in strategic planning is taking a sharper, stronger, and more compelling dimension."

It is right to take a deeper look at values. Some agreements on values, Sonia says, might be just situational or a tool to harmonize differences or tensions. As such, they are useful and contribute, but now we need a more "defining and non-forgiving approach" to identify and operationalize values with a more direct focus on a "non-negotiable" standard. We need statements of what we expect and embrace – as well as statements of what we reject, cannot tolerate, and what we will speak against. And the courage to do so!

Being clear and non-negotiable on your values that relate and reflect your vision is effective to engage stakeholders and collaborators as well as staff, board members, and volunteers. In Sonia's time at American Humane, an organization founded in 1877 that created standards for child welfare, the values were also positions on societal problems and served to galvanize people in many efforts. "We created a business plan that incorporated these values as positions in advocacy, public relations, and speaking out," she says. "The result of building program and fundraising on *strong* values was more success in program and growth of $27 million in six-and-a half years."

Your values define who you are. You should have, as Sonia says, the courage to insist on your values and to speak out against those positions and individuals who fail to reflect those values. When I was doing a leadership training program in a Central European country, I asked the NGO participants to identify individuals who had extraordinary leadership skills. One participate named Adolf Hitler and another person named Joseph Stalin. I was astounded. The two participants argued for their choice by saying that I had asked them to identify individuals with strong leadership skills, and certainly the two men they identified had those skills, to the detriment of millions. I forgot to emphasize the importance of values! Personal values and organizational values! We need to stand up for the *strong* core values we hold, make sure they are for a better world, incorporate them into our programs and advocacy, and insist they are not negotiable with staff, board members, partners, elected officials, and the public.

We often read or hear about individuals who have lost their moral compass, but I believe that you need not only your clear moral compass but also your strong moral backbone. When nonprofits have both the compass and the backbone, they can help develop a more civil society.

Later, I present two levels of values exploration: the first in Chapter 8 as part of the strategic planning process and the second in Chapter 11 as a more thorough approach to values and culture. Organizations that have recently completed a values assessment and smaller organizations can use the short version presented in Chapter 8. The in-depth process in Chapter 11 will be more meaningful for most organizations. Once you are clear about your strong core values, you can address how to identify the organization culture you need to support your strategic plans.

Questions for implementation

1. Does your organization have a clear and strong values statement? Does it address the problems in the world today? Does it help give everyone the courage to speak out for those values in their work?

2. Do you see how strong core values help define your organization and are the basis of your culture? Do your current values invigorate your program services and give you more power in your advocacy and public outreach?

3. Are you ready to conduct the process of addressing your core values during the strategic planning retreat or in a separate session to involve more people? Does your nonprofit need to confirm, clarify, update, or identify your strong core values?

"I'm enjoying our collaboration – and I'm wondering how I can do more."

"Yes, together, we can ensure our strong core values strengthen our program."

5

The significance of organization culture – Overview

Anyone who has traveled knows there is a difference between the cultures of different countries. Japanese culture is different from British culture. Dutch culture is different from Russian culture. American culture is different from Canadian culture. Understanding and respecting a nation's culture is necessary to be able to work well within it. Visitors and new residents in a country are strongly advised to follow the local cultural norms.

Time, for example, is a major cultural differentiator. If the local norm is to start a meeting ten minutes late and you arrive sixty minutes late, you have a problem. If the local norm is to start a meeting sixty minutes late and you arrive fifty minutes early, you have a problem. The problem is not when the meeting actually begins; the problem arises when you do not conform to the local norm. It is culture that determines when meetings really begin.

A well-tuned organization culture gives staff and volunteers a similar way to communicate and behave, which reduces stress and provides the lubricant for getting along.

Culture defines common behavior

Culture is the glue that binds a group together. When the culture is clear and we fit in with it, we are comfortable in that group. We can relax. We can focus and be productive. That's why you often see visitors from another country sticking together in their own group during a tour – they can relax and be comfortable within their own culture. Or why teens hang out together, or why girls or boys or so many other self-selecting groups stick together. In a common culture, behavior is comfortable and free of stress. At work, organization culture unites everyone in what they do, facilitates common pursuit of agreed goals, and prevents undermining of leadership.

Values and culture reflect on each other.

- **Values = Beliefs**
    - o What we hold dear, based on faith and belief
    - o What we must do to live the right way
- **Culture = Behavior**
    - o How we relate, based on reason and emotion
    - o How we want all of us to do things together

How do you understand a society? By looking at its values and culture

Core values come from the history and experience of a country. In a Spanish course I took in Mexico a few years ago, the professor (who had taught language and culture for decades) compared the adjacent cultures of Canada, the United States, and Mexico as guidance on how to behave while in Mexico. He first summarized the key values of Canadian culture as: "We are friendly and orderly, we have good government, and we want to be the peacemakers in the world." The Canadians in the class looked at each other and smiled in agreement. The professor next said that the key values in the United States are: "We believe in liberty, opportunity, and the pursuit of happiness. We want to get ahead and are determined to do that." The Americans in the class looked at each other and grimaced in embarrassed agreement. The professor then said the fundamental values in Mexico are: "We value our personal relationships and family most of all." The Mexicans in the room nodded and smiled warmly at each other.

A society's values influence its culture, which in turn influences behavior. For example, the professor explained that when you go into a small store in Mexico, you should say *"Hola. ¿Cómo estás? ¿Permiso?"* or "Hello. How are you? May I come in?" just as you would if you approached a neighbor's home. This is really beautiful, and it is so different than going into a store in New York City or even Toronto! The values of these three countries are different, and their cultures reflect this.

Understanding the culture you are in is an important guide to your behavior. It enables you to live and work well in that culture. And to arrive at the right time for meetings!

Culture matters: In nations, in corporations, within countries, and in nonprofits

How do you define your national culture compared to the culture of your neighboring countries? Or your group's culture compared to another group? Or your standing in your society? Consider how the differences can cause misunderstandings, missed connections, bad manners, insults, and other more serious disruptions.

If you make small mistakes in another culture and people know where you come from, they may be tolerant and understanding. If they are friends, they'll help you understand how to behave. If you make big mistakes and really cross their values, they will be deeply offended. At worst, a cultural miscommunication or conflict becomes a clash. A clash can be an inconvenience or waste of time, but it can escalate into something seriously disruptive.

Culture is either the "oil" or "sand" in your engine

When there is a conflict of cultures inside an organization, it is like sand in your work that leads to confusion and misunderstandings, personal offense and distraction, and ultimately feuds and failure. When the culture is well-crafted and supports the strategic and operational plans, it is like oil that enables your work to run smoothly and without stalling. Sand or oil will determine how your plans progress.

Organizational success is usually seen as the result of good leaders, good workers, and good plans. This is true, but underlying the leadership, staff, and plans are the organization's values and culture. If they are not carefully considered, articulated, and lived, leadership is not doing its job, workers are confused, and objectives are not achieved. Generally accepted core values and a unified organization culture are the foundation of your nonprofit organization.

Here is an example of core values and unified organization culture. The U.S. Postal Service is a respected domestic federal agency. Its workers are known to be committed to getting the day's mail processed, out the door, and on its way. The agency's culture is embodied in the slogan "Neither snow nor rain nor heat nor gloom of night stays these couriers from the swift completion of their appointed rounds." In my experience, this slogan continues to guide and motivate postal workers.

A remarkable example of the U.S. Postal Service's values and culture occurred 100 years ago. The proposed Nineteenth Amendment to the U.S. Constitution to give women the right to vote needed one more state to vote for ratification. Tennessee was the last state that might possibly ratify the amendment. On August 18, 1920, the Tennessee House of Representatives with the tiniest margin voted to approve and forwarded the bill to Tennessee's governor, the Senate having already given its approval. According to Elaine Weiss in *The Woman's Hour: The Great Fight to Win the Vote*, some states, corporations, manufacturers, liquor interests, railroads, and other anti-suffrage forces engaged in all kinds of efforts to reverse, delay, or otherwise prevent certification of Tennessee's vote.

After overcoming these efforts, the Tennessee governor forwarded the certification papers on August 25 by train and the Postal Service to Washington, D.C. Meanwhile, anti-suffrage forces petitioned a federal court of appeals to delay the ratification (thereby denying women their vote), which would have caused nationwide havoc and protests leading up to the November 1920 elections. The leadership and employees of the Postal Service lived up to their core values and organization culture – they waited for the 4:00 a.m. arrival of the train carrying the certification papers and rushed them to the U.S. Secretary of State. He signed the proclamation of the Nineteenth Amendment early in the morning of August 26, 1920. His signature certified that all conditions for ratification had been met. This act added the amendment to the U.S. Constitution, giving women the right to vote. Strong values and a unified organization culture matter in politics, in corporations, in nonprofits, everywhere – they make things work correctly, the way they should.

Knowing who you are

When I was working with a major nonprofit organization in Belarus, the thirty people in the planning session were mystified when I spoke about organization culture. To help them, I asked them to work in small groups to define their country's national culture. After some time, they identified the following components of their national culture: We are hardworking, we are nice, we like people, and we really don't know who we are. (In the past, this country has been considered part of Russia, and now many people want to be independent.)

After some further discussion and intensive group work, they identified their current organization culture as: hardworking, pleasant, committed, and not yet unified. The undefined culture would have created a problem for the organization if we had not addressed this topic and identified their new culture as hardworking, pleasant, committed, and now unified behind their vision and mission. As I write this in September 2020, we see the people of Belarus as hardworking, pleasant, committed, and unified behind their vision of freedom and democracy after contested elections.

Later in this book, I offer guidance for your team (managers, staff, board members, and critical volunteers) to identify and develop the new, desired culture your organization needs to fulfill your strategic plan and organizational plans.

Questions for implementation

1. In a few words, can you identify the values and culture of your region, city, or neighborhood?

2. Do you personally believe your organization's culture is oil or sand? What will you do about that?

3. Will you be able to lead others to a clear understanding of how strong core values and supporting organization culture influence and even determine your organization's impact?

Will your culture be sand or oil in your plans?

6

Preparation for strong values and supporting culture – Start Now

Good fundraising strategy and good culture reflect and reinforce each other. Nonprofit leaders often tell me, "We had good plans, but they didn't work." I can usually tell them why! Most organizations, for example, need more funding and should recognize they need a better fundraising strategy and a bigger fundraising effort. What's missing? Having a culture that fully supports fundraising. I tell these leaders they need the right organization culture to succeed.

Successfully implementing your new, desired culture can directly – and significantly – increase revenue. For example, as I mentioned earlier in this book, the fundraising efforts of Foster Parents Plan resulted in tripling revenue from $10 million to $30 million in just six years.

Strategic Organization

- ◆ Pulling **all** together toward the same vision
- ◆ Working in the same culture!

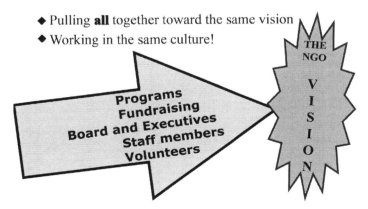

Programs
Fundraising
Board and Executives
Staff members
Volunteers

THE NGO

VISION

Although funding may initially come easily to an organization through grants, this is risky, because grants can suddenly disappear. To grow and have greater program impact, most organizations will eventually make plans for a larger and more diversified fundraising effort. The right culture is needed to support these plans. The right culture is oil in your engine while the wrong culture is sand.

Core values *are the fundamental beliefs that shape how an organization carries out its mission. They are the basis of culture and guide everything you do.* **Organization culture** *is the glue that binds people together and gives them a similar way of behaving. Culture unifies vision, mission, values, goals, strategies, and objectives – and the people – into common behavior.*

In this chapter, we will explore how creating an organization culture that actively supports fundraising – what I call a *fundraising culture* – can support your organization's fundraising plans, strategies, and results. Next, I include suggestions to enhance your organization culture with a robust management style – what I call a management culture – to support effective fundraising. You can build these concepts into your strategic plan, operational plans, and your new, desired culture.

This challenge is for the executive director who wants to increase the significance of the organization, the program director who wants to have more funding for program activities, the finance director who wants to have a more stable and sustainable organization, and of course the fundraising director who wants to succeed in the fundraising challenge. The point is: *Yes, you can do it!* Here are five steps to help.

To build a fundraising culture, get *everyone involved* to support fundraising

A culture that gives serious attention to fundraising by everyone – including program and administrative staff – is more likely to achieve greater fundraising success. Getting everyone involved in supporting fundraising should be reflected in the organization's culture and strategic plan as well as in day-to-day practice.

Throughout my career, I have heard perhaps fifty executive directors complain that they hired a fundraiser who failed to get results in the first year, so the executive director fired that employee. I usually ask, "Well, how did you help? What did the board of directors do to support fundraising efforts? How did everyone support the fundraiser's work? How about the program staff? And the finance/administration staff?" Without an organization-wide culture of fundraising – and without organization-wide support – even good, experienced fundraisers will often fail.

While working in Southeast Asia with the field staff of CARE, a leading international NGO, I was focusing on the need for the program staff to develop a deep commitment to fundraising as well as to their program responsibilities. I have often seen in NGOs that program staff can have a dislike of dealing with donors – after all, they joined the organization for its mission and work, not to raise money.

After some discussion, I was pleased when a young field coordinator said to everyone else, *"Oh, I get it. Fundraising – it's my job."* By that he meant fundraising support was part of his responsibility as a member of the organization. In that moment, he also recognized that fundraising produced the income to pay his salary, implement the program he helped to deliver, and provide services to program beneficiaries. He saw that he played an important role in fundraising by providing top-notch reports, adding stories and photographs he thought donors would like, welcoming donors for field visits, and of course getting excellent program results.

"Fundraising – it's my job" can be an internal slogan for everyone at any nonprofit organization. This phrase emphasizes the importance of fundraising as an organization-wide strategy, helps to create a culture that supports fundraising, and incorporates appropriate fundraising responsibilities into everyone's job responsibilities and performance review.

To build a fundraising culture, *think ahead* to see financial needs in five or more years

Planning the fundraising effort as an investment and long-term proposition is far more likely to succeed than treating it as a single-year effort. This is another concept that leads to clear plans, better strategy, and stronger culture to support fundraising for the results it will produce.

Based on personal experience, I know it is necessary to present the fundraising budget as investment in a multi-year plan with a return in revenues in future years rather than simply as a portion of the annual budget of revenue and expenditure. Generally, board members and heads of other departments will often see a one-year fundraising budget as providing insufficient return in that year and, therefore, view the fundraising budget as taking funds away from the program. Fundraising expenditures can only be justified as investments in future revenues. Again and again, I have seen that the finance director and board treasurer are more likely to understand concepts of investment in fundraising as important for growth and sustainability.

Fundraising as a long term investment vs fundraising as a one year expense

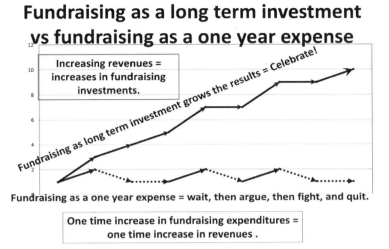

Increasing revenues = increases in fundraising investments.

Fundraising as long term investment grows the results = Celebrate!

Fundraising as a one year expense = wait, then argue, then fight, and quit.

One time increase in fundraising expenditures = one time increase in revenues .

Consider this situation: In the 1990s and early 2000s, there was a huge flow of foreign funding to support new NGOs in Eastern and Central Europe. The funding came from government aid agencies and international foundations seeking to respond to serious needs in society and to support the development of civil society. This funding was valuable and effective for many years – until those funding agencies and foundations turned their attention to other regions and other issues. In the U.S., the situation is similar for organizations supported by government contracts – until suddenly they are not – as a result of a change in politics, legislation, or other priorities.

In both situations, nonprofits will go out of business if they have not prepared or developed other sustainable funding sources. It takes three years (or more) to develop a sustainable funding flow from new methods and new categories in fundraising. The best time to explore and initiate new fundraising efforts is before you need them. An organization culture that is forward thinking and understands the importance of fundraising as a long-term investment is key for organizational growth and sustainability.

To build a fundraising culture, *build organizational capacity* for fundraising

The cost in time and money for an organization to get a few grants is far less than the effort needed to have a sustainable and diversified fundraising program. Accordingly, an organization that wants to secure and increase its future funding should build capacity – the commitment, skills, and knowledge of staff and board members – to engage in fundraising efforts.

Realistically, this is at least a three-year effort to expand the thinking and increase staff and board skills and experience. Capacity building is among the most important responsibilities of an organization's leadership. New staff with specialized skills may be required. New board members with good fundraising connections and willingness to fundraise are probably needed. The commitment by the organization's leaders, both executive and board, to grow the organization's financial resources is necessary, and it requires new thinking, new plans, new strategy, and new culture to manage a far more complex organization and fundraising effort.

Fundraising capacity includes the ability of executives, fundraising staff, board members, and other volunteers to:

- Understand the principles of fundraising and how to appeal to donors.
- Plan, strategize, implement, and evaluate the various methods of fundraising.
- Understand their roles and responsibilities to make a donor-attractive organization.
- Identify, involve, and support major donors, special advisors, and national figures.
- Identify profiles of individuals, new groups, and other entities responsive to your appeals.

- Research, approach, and involve local and national governments and corporations.
- Conduct marketing in traditional mass media and social media to recruit new donors.
- Attract and support needed volunteers to expand your work and reduce your costs.
- Strengthen your board of directors and create an honorary board to support fundraising.

To build a fundraising culture, *increase effort* in staff time and budget for fundraising

An essential step to success is to understand that an increased effort in fundraising is needed to produce increased results. In nonprofit organizations, as in for-profit businesses, it takes money to raise money. A culture that prioritizes fundraising will support increased staff effort and budget allocation in this area.

At Foster Parents Plan, after presenting good results in marketing tests, we were able to show the board that a significant increase in the fundraising budget would enable us to increase the long-term program funding significantly, even though a temporary decrease in program expenditures would be needed. In other words, we proposed reducing the program budget to increase the fundraising budget in the short-term in order to increase the program budget far more over the long-term. The board agreed to the higher fundraising budget and allocated even more for the fundraising effort with a loan from the reserve fund.

The fundraising department was able to repay the loan quite quickly from increased revenues, and we were able to fund both the fundraising and program functions at substantially increased levels for years after that. Now, thirty years later, the resulting increase in continuing contributions is still supporting the organization's work.

When I facilitated the strategic planning process at the Medicines for Malaria Venture, the finance director was the strongest advocate for increased spending in fundraising. He saw the expected results from the three-year fundraising plan and endorsed the "fundraising as investment" approach with the business-minded board and staff members. The organization's new fundraising culture that we had put in place facilitated this kind of thinking by everyone involved. This led to increases in the fundraising effort, which generated more funding for program work over the long term. As a result, the organization was able to expand its program significantly and, subsequently, have a greater program impact.

To build a fundraising culture, dedicate *serious attention* to identify, support, and live the new culture

It is not easy to change culture, especially in a larger organization. It is far easier to change written plans than to change people's behavior. In addressing organization culture, the nonprofit's leaders must be adept in managing the change. People will resist change, especially if it is abruptly done without consultation or supporting systems.

In my experience, I've found that it is important to manage culture change very carefully. This is best done as part of the strategic planning process. In any organization, I would present culture as an essential means to achieve the results the team just identified in the planning process. Involving everyone in the culture planning step is important, both to get it right and to get full commitment.

Addressing the culture discussion within a three-day strategic planning retreat works well for small and medium-size organizations. For a neighborhood association, this could be the focus of a regular meeting, taking an hour or so. For a larger organization, I suggest a half-day gathering after the retreat so more staff (or at least more representatives) could participate.

To identify the culture you need, I recommend leading the discussion with the organization's inspiring vision, empowering mission, and strong values. Then focus on managing for results and demonstrate how the right culture facilitates everyone's success. (Talking about "achieving the results you want based on your plans" is far more effective than talking about changing anyone's behavior.)

Next, you can begin the process of working on culture as described later in this book. The key is for staff to experience any new culture as something that flows logically from the new strategic plan – something they help to define – and that enables them to be more successful in achieving the expected results they support.

Another technique to establish new culture is identifying a cheerleading squad – a team of individuals who remind everyone of the new culture and support efforts to live it. Other supporting techniques include discussions in staff meetings, awards for great performance, signs in hallways and offices, individual action plans, and performance appraisals.

It is especially important for the organization's leaders to model and promote the desired culture. A frequent reminder to all staff when I was at the International Federation of Red Cross and Red Crescent Societies, for example, was to "Walk the talk."

Your organization's new fundraising culture needs to be consistently demonstrated and continuously reinforced.

How to build a good *management culture* for all functions

In addition to the steps for building and supporting fundraising culture presented above, I endorse four management concepts or ways of doing business that will support the fundraising effort as well as other functions in your organization. The following paragraphs present advice based on my years of consulting with countless nonprofit organizations around the world.

Management cultures that focus on *solutions* are more successful

Solution thinking is a pathway to future success. This approach has been proven in organization after organization. It can be easy for an organization to get stuck in current and recurring problems, problem analysis, and problem thinking.

How do you behave?	PROBLEM THINKING? − − − − −	SOLUTION THINKING! + + + + +
What do you talk about?	Problems! Who's to blame?	Results! How to achieve them?
What do you focus on?	The past and what's wrong now.	The future and what we can do.
Responses to a new idea?	It won't work! Maybe, but...	Let's figure it out. We'll do it!
What are your feelings?	Frustrated. Negative! Ugh!	Energetic. Positive! Yea!
What's happening?	Nothing new! Stagnation.	Positive new things! Innovation.
What are your results?	Continuing what failed.	Building the future.

Solution thinking becomes self-fulfilling. If you focus on problems, you only see problems. If you focus on solutions, you move from problem to action and then from action to success. The new culture for my neighborhood association moved from complaint to challenge, from challenge to opportunity, and from opportunity to a plan of action that empowered the community. I am so proud to see the many activities, the wide support, and the many successes of that association.

Management cultures that focus on excellence are more effective

Excellence is obvious, but it is worthwhile to focus on excellence as a priority in your organization. Organizations that focus on excellence get better results.

In his book *In Pursuit of Excellence* based on a review of highly successful corporations, Tom Peters identifies five essential similarities in culture that he concludes led to their success. Excellence in these five behaviors is equally relevant to nonprofit organizations in their fundraising, program, management, and other functions. The five traits of excellence he identified are:

- Bias toward action
- Close to the customer
- Entrepreneurship
- Tolerance of failure
- Quick feedback

Management cultures that practice *positive thinking* are more productive

This is equally obvious, but it is also worthwhile to focus on positive thinking as a priority in your organization. Organizations that practice positive thinking will get better results.

I am guided deeply by Dr. Martin Luther King's "dream" speech. I built my professional dream on his dream, with words like, "We will all be at the top of the mountain together, men and women, young and old, black and white, donors and fundraisers, government and business, everyone united to make this a better world."

In a workshop for NGO executives from countries with a tradition of powerlessness and negative thinking, I was encouraging the participants rather passionately to adopt new thinking and new attitudes. They were skeptical in our sessions but eventually wanted to agree. In a closing dinner, they put on a short skit with a large map of a country with a wide river dividing it in half. They showed themselves and their organizations on one side of the map, full of problems and no solutions, while I was on the other side of the river jumping up and down and shouting about positive thinking. At the end of their skit, the narrator presented this conclusion, "Ken has been telling us all these days about the many bridges to get to the other side of the river where we can find solutions, progress, and success, but we all know from experience that there have been no bridges but only barriers where we live." After a few minutes of silence, everyone concluded with smiles and a standing applause. These leaders appreciated their new insight into the attitudes I shared about positive thinking and, later, they made it clear that they were planning to adopt this new way of thinking.

I find power in sayings and proverbs that reinforce optimism and positive thinking. Here are just a few, and you can find more from your country and culture:

- "When one door shuts, a hundred open." – Spanish proverb
- "When you see a rattlesnake poised to strike, strike first."
  – Native American proverb
- "The smallest stump can overturn the largest carriage."
  – Romanian proverb
- "Optimism is a tonic. Pessimism is poison."
  – B.C. Forbes, founder of *Forbes* magazine
- "You must do the thing you think you cannot do."
  – Eleanor Roosevelt (She dreamed of a universal declaration of human rights and worked to make that dream come true.)

Management cultures that focus on *important issues* are more efficient

Research highlights how much time in most offices is wasted on activities that are not important. Staff in nonprofits can also waste time on activities that appear to be urgent but are, in fact, not really important. It is hard to put aside an activity or a responsibility that seems urgent, so a culture that promotes doing the important rather than the urgent is key to organizational efficiency, effectiveness, and results. It may appear self-evident that a maximum amount of staff time should be dedicated to activities that are important, but this needs to be emphasized!

In our daily work, most of us are faced with far more tasks and challenges than it is possible to accomplish. We often choose the urgent tasks, because it seems they must be done right away, and it feels good to check off accomplished tasks. However, many urgent tasks are not important at all! For these, there is no loss if you simply ignore them. Most people can increase their output or productivity by ignoring the many tasks that are not important and focusing only on the important tasks. This is a question of judgment.

Good planning and the right culture significantly reduce the time people waste on urgent but unimportant tasks by encouraging and supporting everyone to address the important and probably more difficult issues first, on a priority basis.

Here is an example of focusing on the important and getting it done effectively and quickly. I know a board member who can accomplish more in a ten-minute phone call than most people would take far more time to do. He had a file in which he kept key information about everyone he met – work, family, interests, concerns, and stories. In the first minute of a call, he would ask about your daughter's graduation, your recent golf tournament, or your mother's health.

Then he'd jump to the point of the call, offer several reasons the person should agree to his offer or request, and conclude with appreciation and warm wishes to the family. He was sincere, and others appreciated his clarity and directness – and usually welcomed his request. This is

+ + + + + **IMPORTANT AND URGENT**	+ + + + + **IMPORTANT BUT NOT URGENT**
Spend your FIRST time here. • Aligning and building teams • Planning and monitoring • Deadline-driven projects • Resolving real problems • Preventing problems • Decision meetings • Listening	*Spend MOST of your time here.* • Communicating vision and mission • Mentoring and supporting staff • Building organization culture • Reaching out to stakeholders • Strengthening the board • Building relationships • Developing your skills

– – – – **NOT IMPORTANT BUT URGENT**	– – – – **NOT IMPORTANT AND NOT URGENT**
Spend NO time here. • Many "pressing" matters • Most interruptions • Long phone calls • Small problems • Busywork	*Spend NO time here.* • Secondary matters • Most long reports • Routine meetings • Detailed emails • Office gossip

a simple example of how focusing on the important can be extremely productive and efficient.

As an executive, I used to glance at incoming mail, email, and reports and put them into three piles – a first pile of important for action today, a second in a top drawer for later consideration, and a third in a bottom drawer for even later. I took care of the first pile and would review some of the papers in the first drawer to see if they were important enough to warrant prompt action. I generally never got to the lower drawer! This approach allowed me to focus on important tasks, projects, and decisions.

The existing and often entrenched organization culture can be good or bad

A nonprofit's culture is good when it enables your organization to operate smoothly, efficiently, effectively, and pleasantly; everyone is in sync and works together for success. It is bad when entrenched culture undercuts your plans, when people don't live up to expectations, or when conflicts from subcultures arise. It is ugly when the culture permits exploitation, corruption, or violence.

- **Good.** When I asked the executive director of a small Romanian organization with just five staff members about culture, she identified the culture as: professional, responsible, having integrity, focused on results, and empowering. She added that they have a rigorous selection process for new staff involving everyone in the hiring decision and a focus on developing people once they are on board. This sounded pretty good to me, and having seen the organization in action, I can attest that everyone lives this culture. The culture had never been articulated so precisely, but I'm convinced that it was communicated by conversation, example, and practice on a day-by-day basis. In a small, close-knit organization, this is possible. However, in most organizations, it is necessary to articulate the desired culture in writing.

- **Bad.** The statement of a big international airline on expected behavior includes: "Listen closely and communicate openly, honestly, and directly; embrace diverse people, thinking, and styles; treat each other with dignity and respect; demand and accept responsibility; and follow through with clear, consistent consequences." How great these words are, and how I wish they were followed every time I experienced problems while traveling and encountered terrible customer service.

Nonprofit organizations are *distinctive* in being formed to make this a better world

The vision for any nonprofit should be inspiring, the mission empowering, and the values determining. Together vision, mission, and values are the essential components to find solutions, assure excellence, think positive, and focus on important matters to achieve success. A strong management culture supports fundraising, program, and all other functions in the organization.

When the five concepts for "fundraising culture" and the four concepts for "management culture" are woven into the organization's strategic plan, the desired organization culture, and day-to-day practice, there is better management, better attitude, better staff work, and better results.

To review, the recommendations to build a good "fundraising culture" are:

1. Everyone supports the fundraising effort. "That's my job!"
2. We understand fundraising is a long-term investment for increased funding.
3. We build the capacity of board members, executives, and staff for fundraising.
4. We increase our efforts and budget to increase fundraising results.
5. We live our strong fundraising culture.

The recommendations to build a good "management culture" include:

1. We are solution-oriented and reject problem thinking.
2. We strive to achieve excellence in everything we do.
3. We are positive thinkers and are passionate about our vision and mission.
4. We focus on important tasks to achieve the desired results.

The biggest NGOs are growing faster – What can you do?

In case you have any reservations about what I have written thus far in this book, I want to share what I see happening in the NGO world. The number of NGOs is growing but, more significantly for NGO leaders, organizations are consolidating, just as in the corporate world. Approximately the top 20% of nonprofits are thriving and growing; they are securing ever larger shares of philanthropy and making significant improvements in society. The next 20% of NGOs are working hard to maintain their positions, their revenues, and their futures; most of them will do well and continue to contribute to society. The middle 20% of NGOs are seriously struggling, and the lower 40% of NGOs are at considerable risk of disappearing or continuing to maintain a low level of services. Just as in the corporate world, the largest NGOs are getting larger, and the smaller ones are having a more difficult time surviving.

To survive, a significant majority of NGOs need a better planning process, strong values and a supporting culture that fuel their ability to grow and have more impact, and more collaboration with other nonprofits. There are just too many surveys and reports about NGOs not having good planning, not earning donor trust, not managing professionally, not supporting fundraising staff, and not getting the needed new board members. This all comes down to good leadership at all levels in the organization, all staff understanding the fundamental principles of fundraising, and excellent strategic plans with a supporting culture. The answers are here and in my first book, *Make a Better World*.

Questions for implementation

1. What are some ways you can build a "fundraising culture" in your organization, so everyone – in all functions – has an active role in supporting fundraising?

2. What are some ways you can build a "management culture" in your organization, so everyone (at all levels) is solution-oriented, strives for excellence, is passionate about the vision and mission, and stays focused on the important tasks?

3. Can you talk or meet with contacts from other nonprofits to learn how they address values and culture? If so, can you make a list of those organizations and start working with (and building) this network?

4. Now is the time to get people thinking about these issues. What can YOU do right now to begin the process to create strong core values and the supporting culture for growth and success?

"Where do we go from here?   "Let's plan! Let's innovate!"
Where are we now?"

PART III

Let's do it –
Creating strategic and
operational plans
for success

In Part I, you read an overview of strategic and operational planning. In Part II, you read an overview of the importance of strong core values and a supporting organization culture. Now in Part III, it's time to go to work!

The next three chapters guide you to develop the strategic and operational plans for your nonprofit or community association. I recommend that most nonprofits conduct the planning work over several days of meetings, for example, a three-day strategic planning retreat. Community associations can address the planning activities over several hours in several well-planned meetings.

Good planning is based on the realities (research) facing you along with creativity (new ideas) and innovation (new actions). It is essential that you complete both the internal research and external research before you begin your planning sessions.

When you have the results of all internal and external research as presented in Part I, then you are ready for the planning retreat. Usually an off-site retreat is best for participation, process, and outputs, because people will not be distracted and will focus on the planning. Relaxed time together including evenings will produce a better result for both teambuilding and planning.

Now, in the next three chapters, we turn to *what you do when you get to the actual strategic planning retreat.* The planning is in four steps:

1. Exploring the realities of the world and imagining the possibilities
2. Drafting the essential elements of your strategic plan
3. Drafting your detailed operational plans
4. Planning the follow up and implementation

Good planning is a balance between realistic assessments and imagining new possibilities. I always seek a mix of fact and fancy! The facts come from the research and analysis, and the fancy comes from creative brainstorming and imagining new possibilities. The two work together like yin and yang to create a new reality by stretching participants' thinking to new levels of achievement, while still grounded in reality.

The work in planning flows:

- From understanding reality based on the research findings and what donors want from you plus the dreaming and brainstorming about what you really might be able to achieve;

- To considering and drafting the eight key elements of your strategic directions including vision, mission, values, goals, strategies, image, trust, and culture;

- Then to operationalizing the strategic directions into detailed plans of action for what each functional area, team, and individual could actually achieve.

As you may recall in earlier chapters, some of the research questions asked respondents to identify their hopes and dreams for the organization and its work. These aspirations should be reflected in the reports presented during the strategic planning retreat. In addition, several brainstorming sessions during the retreat will focus on letting participants share their dreams for beneficiaries as well as their highest aspirations for funding, for program, and for the organization as a whole.

As social entrepreneurs, you are working for a better world, so you should think smart and think big. Fact and fancy. Reality and innovation.

I encourage you to download and print the planning tools, checklists, and detailed worksheets from my website (www.NGOFutures.com), which will be useful as you lead the planning. Follow the guidance in this book and use these tools, and the outcome will be strong strategic and operational plans that empower your organization to build on past achievements, correct weaknesses, and move forward with challenging and stretching plans.

The next three chapters describe in detail what you *actually do* during the strategic planning process.

Design thinking

A lot has been written about design thinking in the past decade. An article in the *Princeton Alumni Weekly* in October 2020 defined design thinking as "a human-centered, collaborative, creative mindset that begins with open-ended questions rather than a clearly defined hypothesis." In *Health Design Thinking*, Dr. Bon Ku and Ellen Lupton call it a human-centered perspective that "starts with the needs and desires of people, rather than with a business proposition or an artistic idea" and a creative mindset "favoring open-ended exploration." Design thinking is what successful NGOs regularly do in their strategic planning – involvement of the team, reality-based research, assessment of stakeholders, and innovative thinking, all strategically planned (designed) to work best for key stakeholders. Design thinking is good NGO strategic planning – it should be embraced with all the elements described in this book.

I've utilized these elements in my work and consulting for decades. In March 2020, I presented a lecture on leadership and fundraising in a "design thinking" professional course for NGOs in Mexico. You can find it on my website.

7

Understanding realities and imagining possibilities – Day One

The work of the first day flows from understanding the realities through the background and research findings in the morning to expanding your horizons through visioning and brainstorming in the afternoon. This is the needed preparation for your strategic planning the next day. The first day is also about getting people to feel comfortable with each other, which is important, because people from different functions will be analyzing information and participating in decisions about other departments – honest assessment, attentive listening, mutual respect, and good feelings are needed. It is important to get people away from their daily pressures.

The work of the first day of the retreat is to develop a clear understanding of the realities facing the organization and to think creatively about future possibilities. The work builds on all the research completed before the sessions.

The following timeline is approximate, and you should manage the time according to your own situation. Most NGOs will need a full day for this. A small organization or community group should address each of the following steps by doing them in shorter, simpler, and easier ways.

I encourage you to refer to the template agenda for a three-day strategic planning retreat in Appendix 3. You should make a copy of those pages for reference as you prepare your own agenda to present the following action steps.

Plan a session on teambuilding (one hour at the beginning or the evening before)

Start with a teambuilding activity in which participants have the space to relax and interact. If this is a new group of participants who do not work together regularly, it is quite important to open with some team-building activities to create relationships of openness and trust. Even if everyone knows each other, some teambuilding is useful.

The best teambuilding activity I have seen is to gather the group the evening before for a reception or dinner with an introduction and welcome along with some informal discussion on a general topic of importance. This step will help to ensure people participate positively and productively.

I suggest this theme: "Everyone working together for success! How can we do it?" Alternatively, you can do the "Change versus status quo" activity that I include on my website. This activity enables everyone to see the validity and necessity to keep some elements in your work as they are and to change others to break new ground.

Open with a review of expectations for the retreat (one-half hour maximum)

Gather everyone in the planning group to review why you are having the retreat and what you want to produce during these days. Present the expectations for the retreat including process and expected results. Distribute the worksheets so everyone has a copy. Review the agenda, present the detail for the sessions, and ask for any questions for clarification. Emphasize that it is vitally important to build the strategic plan and operational plans on reality, creativity, and "blue sky" thinking. Also: no cell phones, no emails, no distractions.

How will you capture information, questions, and conclusions? The organizing team should have made clear plans to capture the work of the sessions.

The *facilitator* is responsible to get good participation, keep the meetings on schedule, and get the group to reach conclusions. The facilitator or consultant, if you have one, is there to guide the process, assure honest discussion, and provide counsel as you go along.

A *reporter* or "idea catcher" lists and records in a PowerPoint slide (or on a flip chart) the major points and conclusions, both good and bad, from reports and discussions to keep these top of mind as you conduct the planning. The facilitator and reporter should always be looking for possible improvements for your plans in two key areas:

1. The *key roles* or *attributes* of nonprofits (promoting the cause, providing services, educating, advocating, independent voice, and nonprofit status). Are you doing these well? How can you do better?

2. The *essential responsibilities* of nonprofits (value to society, results achieved, efficiency in operations, trustworthiness in behavior, and accountability to stakeholders). Are you doing and communicating these well? How can you do better?

Meanwhile, all participants should keep a running list of issues and concerns to address plus any ideas for consideration in their specific areas of responsibility:

1. What improvements are possible in programs or services, fundraising or marketing, and finance or administration?

2. What about staffing and teamwork? Governance, leadership, and management?

3. What do we need to improve in our culture, trustworthiness, and positioning?

4. What about promotion, outreach, volunteers, education, and advocacy?

5. How can we plan, keep track of progress, and get better results?

6. How else can we organize ourselves to produce better results?

7. What other issues need to be addressed?

Finally, *one person* (possibly the reporter) is assigned to capture in PowerPoint (or on a flip chart) the major conclusions for what will become part of your strategic plan document. This facilitates agreement on final wording of key strategic statements when participants actually *see* the wording as they go along and also captures the final version of the plan itself.

Present the findings from research (two to three hours)

These high-level oral reports on findings and conclusions should be brief, with one to two pages in writing in summary bullet points. The reports and recommendations are presented and discussed only for clarification. The emphasis is on establishing a firm basis of reality and sharing lessons from various sources. The logical flow of reports, *which you have completed before the planning,* is:

1. *History* for a common view of accomplishments, challenges, precedents, and progress

2. *Lessons learned* from evaluations and reports to provide the basis for planning

3. *Findings from surveys* of participants, donors, partners, authorities, staff, and others

4. *Competitor and partner assessments* and recommendations
5. *Current donor group* assessment as background
6. *Program* report with survey findings, analysis, and recommendations
7. *Fundraising* report with survey findings, analysis, and recommendations
8. *Finance* report with survey findings, analysis, and recommendations
9. *Findings and recommendations* by the consultant for guidance based on what others think
10. *Current strategic plan* insights to assure a good and successful planning process

The written results from this research should be available for guidance, inspiration, and reference during the strategic planning and after the plans are created.

Look broadly at the landscape (during the lunch break)

Look at the landscape: What is changing? What is new? This is a panel discussion presented by several external experts who share insights into the outside landscape the organization will face in the coming few years. Addressing this topic works well as a panel discussion during the lunch break.

I first saw use of "What is the landscape in your field of expertise?" with a global organization working in antibiotic resistance. For the planning session, we invited experts from government, foundations, business, and healthcare to share their views. It was a productive and eye-opening experience that contributed much to the planning.

I suggest you invite three to five outside experts to share their thoughts on developments in the social, environmental, economic, political, technological, media, and marketing fields. These presenters could be selected from advertising or public relations agencies, management consultants, university or government officials, board members, or others whose experience and wisdom you respect. It is an informal session focused on opportunities and threats for program, funding, and management.

I would ask the panel members to address these questions:

- "What do you, as an expert in your field, see coming our way?"
- "What is important for us to know as we plan for the next three (five) years?"

When you invite them, ask them to make a short five-minute contribution and be willing to respond to questions. Be clear that this is not a long discussion or speech. It is a "snap review" of what the future might hold as input into the strategic planning process. Inviting professionals to help for just one short session is also a good way to get them more involved in your organization's work.

R11 WORKSHEET: THE LANDSCAPE WE FACE

What is the landscape we will encounter? Emerging results in our field?

Note: Five minutes maximum for each panelist, plus time to answer questions

1. Changes we may see in society, politics, and the economy
2. Predictions about possible changes affecting programs
3. Cutting-edge developments in marketing and fundraising
4. Ideas about applications of new technology and social media
5. Recommendations on other issues

Plans for the afternoon

In a retreat, I like to move from *rational sessions* such as looking at the landscape by external experts to *creative sessions* such as sharing dreams in order to stimulate unconstrained thinking by participants.

Given the state of the world and our needs today, you will surely be aiming at significantly higher results in the plans you intend to develop. Most organizations want or need to achieve substantial growth in their revenues, and that will require substantial changes in goals, strategies, plans, and culture. An open-thinking process is more likely to improve the overall plan and will certainly involve participants more fully in implementation of the plan.

The creative sessions in the afternoon will be:

1. Opening up to dreams and aspirations based on visionary thinking
2. Identifying donors and other stakeholders and assessing what they want from you
3. Brainstorming desired long-term results based on the work you might be able to do

Open up to your dreams as visionaries (one hour)

Brainstorm to open up to your dreams: What excites you the most? What are the *ultimate* possibilities for the organization? This is a facilitated session of individual and group work with an emphasis on imagination, even fantasy, with no restraints and no boundaries. The goal is to get participants to create a list of dreams, hopes, or wishes that motivate and inspire them. It is true visionary thinking! This exercise helps participants to be more innovative in their rational thinking activities later in the planning process.

Based on my experience with many nonprofits, I know the value of thinking out of the box, looking for breakthrough ideas, sharing impossible (but maybe possible) dreams, and being visionaries to open up your future.

As you go through the process, look for the big concepts that can guide your organization into the future five or ten years from now – or even longer. The simple way to open people's thinking is to lead a group discussion to address: "What are your dreams for the organization? Be free to say what you feel! Don't put any limits on your hopes and aspirations. What is your vision of what we ultimately could do?"

Ask each person to identify and write down, in just a few words, one or more dreams or wishes that fulfill the ideals of the organization. Tell everyone to put away their internal censor in these dreams. Then ask people to share, one by one, a dream, a hope, an aspiration. Create a list of visionary ideas and possibilities captured in a few words each. Don't let people criticize or be negative about someone else's dreams. Make it fun and encourage laughter. You could share some of your own dreams to get things started.

Here are some questions to ask to get the ideas flowing:

- What are your dreams and aspirations for our organization?
- What visions can you suggest? Utopian achievements?
- What is your most compelling hope for our future?

Keep going with wild ideas, funny suggestions, idealistic thoughts – see how many you can get. Capture the ideas on a PowerPoint slide or flip chart.

The output from this exercise is, quite simply, a list of dreams, aspirations, and wishes spontaneously identified by the planning group participants. As many as twenty or thirty dreams should be captured on PowerPoint slides for projection or on a flip chart, which participants can refer to throughout the strategic planning retreat.

Examples of dreams and aspirations of other organizations

1. The National Center for Healthy Housing expanded its focus from eliminating lead paint in housing to all hazards in the house and, later, to the need for environmentally healthy homes. More recently, the organization expanded its focus to healthy neighborhoods. The dream was to address all health hazards that kids face as they grow up. The dream: "A healthy neighborhood for all children" as *"You can't have a healthy house in an unhealthy neighborhood."*

2. The Ukrainian Down Syndrome Organization expanded its focus from being a grant-funded service to an advocacy and parent support organization. The hope was to become a strong national organization to pressure government, corporations, and everyone else in the country to provide the best support in education, healthcare, and employment for people with Down syndrome. The dream: *"I want my child to grow up to be educated, have a job, and maybe even find love."*

3. West Broadway Neighborhood Association grew from a small homeowner's association to become a more

comprehensive neighborhood improvement association. The wish was to make our neighborhood the best place to live in the city for everyone in its diverse population. The dream: *"Let's be the best neighborhood in the city."*

4. For GreeningRozzie, a community environmental organization which a few friends and I started in Roslindale, Massachusetts (where I live), we convened a community meeting and brainstormed about how green our village could become. This led to identifying the vision, mission, and eight program areas of the organization. The dream was to create a green place to live and raise kids: *"I want to live in a green community."*

5. The NYC Kids Project built on its school program to think about programs in other cities, other countries, and eventually on television and the Internet to spread its message to ever-larger audiences. The dream is to reach all society with its message of tolerance: *"Hey, George, you're in a wheelchair, but in so many ways you and I are just alike. Let's be friends!"*

When I was executive director at Foster Parents Plan, I was the visionary leader looking for breakthroughs and great leaps forward. The director of finance and administration was the realistic manager. It was the combination of breakthrough thinking and realistic planning that enabled the organization to make dramatic progress in the next six years. She recently said to me, "We often disagreed, but we kept talking and always found a way that was both breakthrough and achievable!"

Some organizations have used a method called appreciative inquiry, which is an opening and affirming process. Appreciative inquiry and "opening up to your dreams" as described here are useful expanding steps in pointing to new and positive directions, but they are only first steps and will require more rigorous and realistic analysis. Participants at this stage need not worry that they are being unrealistic or absurd. These ideas are intended to stretch your realistic planning later in the retreat. (You can learn more about the appreciate inquiry method at www.CenterForAppreciativeInquiry.net.)

R12 WORKSHEET: OUR DREAMS AND ASPIRATIONS

What are our dreams?

You need to know everyone's dreams, hopes, and most wishful thoughts. Think openly, creatively, and out of the box. Your dreams should be inspiring and, if achieved, would certainly make your nonprofit famous. (Just keep listing them.)

What are our dreams? Our most optimistic thoughts?

1. _____

2. _____

3. _____

+ _____

Identify stakeholders and what they want from you (one to two hours)

The next creative step is to identify current and potential stakeholders who provide resources for your work. Think through what you want from them, identify what they want from you, and indicate what you must do to satisfy them.

Who are your stakeholders? You should consider who is important to your success both currently and potentially. At the most obvious level, who do you really need to be involved and supportive of your work for your organization to succeed? At a second level, who would be helpful to be involved and supportive? Your stakeholders are the people, groups, institutions, and anyone else who is currently or potentially important for your success.

Stakeholders include current and potential individual donors, prospective major donors, grant makers, partners, corporate executives, and government officials who can support you as well as journalists, writers, celebrities, and others who can influence what others think of your organization. And don't neglect board members, advisors, advocates, critics, evaluators, and suppliers. And certainly, don't forget to include volunteers, staff, and participants in your programs, all of whom in various ways are donors by contributing their time and effort. Note, however, that I believe the three most important stakeholder groups are donors, program participants, and staff/volunteers.

Understanding and responding to stakeholders is an essential rule for fundraising, program, and organizational success. Stakeholder analysis establishes a solid grounding in reality and provides valuable information and perspectives for later work in fundraising, program, and management. Without stakeholder satisfaction, an organization cannot survive, much less grow.

Your important stakeholders are those people and entities who give you something such as money, time, participation, advice, work, endorsement, or something else of value and, as such, they are all valued donors!

Take time to understand what donors want from you, what program participants want from you, and what other groups want from you. It is vitally important to explore and understand *correctly* the answers to these questions:

- Who are your stakeholders?
- What do you really want from your stakeholders?
- What do your stakeholders really want from you?
- How do you know you are providing what they want?

This is detailed group work with feedback and consensus to develop a comprehensive list of stakeholders, what you want from them, what they want from you, and how you know you provide it. You should be open-minded and expansive when considering all of your current and potential stakeholders. I suggest a full group session with the participants calling out categories and individual names to be added to the list on a PowerPoint slide or flip chart. After identifying stakeholders by broad categories such as individual donors, corporations, participants, authorities, and the media, you can refine the assessment by considering subcategories such as major donors and lapsed donors and even a specific company, the mayor, and the local TV station. Don't forget celebrities and sports figures, parents and neighbors, evaluation agencies and nonprofit partners, and anyone else who could be important to your organization. Make the list so people can see the suggestions and add more. Be sure to include partners who can share.

After you have a reasonably long master list, I find it most productive to have small groups of three to four participants working together for forty-five to sixty minutes. You can ask each group to address several different categories of stakeholders. Each group adds new names to its lists and enters the details for what you want from them, what they want from you, and how you know you provide it. It is easy for most organizations to determine what you want from donors and other supporters: money, volunteers, services, materials, free publicity, advice, endorsements, time, and so forth. More challenging – and more important – are the steps to *identify what they want from you and how you can satisfy them.*

This is important, because you need to be attractive and responsive to your stakeholders. Nobody is going to give you anything if they get nothing in return. You need to use your imagination and creativity to identify benefits you can provide to various stakeholders. The more specific you can be, the more likely you are to succeed. No one helps an organization that is not appealing and not responsive. You need to be a "donor attractive" and responsive organization to earn their support.

For these small work groups, it is best to have a mix of participants from different departments in each group to provide a useful variety of viewpoints. Participants from departments not directly involved with a given stakeholder group can contribute valuable perspective and insight and often gain appreciation of the challenges of working with such groups. Participants from program contribute much to the donor discussion, fundraisers contribute to program assessments, finance people contribute to both fundraising and programs, and everyone contributes to management and finance analysis.

After each group captures details in a list on a laptop or worksheets, related lists are later combined into one document, which is given to the relevant department with responsibility for that set of stakeholders as a basis for further planning. For example, a detailed assessment of different categories of donors can form the basis of a more robust fundraising plan of action.

Having high regard for your stakeholders is a key strategy for organizational success. Organizations that neglect their stakeholders are soon in deep trouble!

Real examples of how organizations used their stakeholder assessments to expand programs and fundraising

1. The National Center for Healthy Housing attracted new donors by expanding its range of services that were of interest to potential donors.
2. The Ukrainian Down Syndrome Organization reached out to more parents, families, and local governments to enable parents to get better conditions for their children.
3. The WBNA neighborhood association connected with other residents not currently involved and gave them a voice in their neighborhood.
4. GreeningRozzie showed how every home and every family could play a role in creating a greener community for the benefit of all.
5. NYC Kids Project identified potential new donors and volunteers and let them know they are contributing to a more tolerant and supportive world.
6. At InterAction, the leading American NGOs working globally joined together, recognizing the power of collaboration.

If you are expanding your program services, think about new stakeholders who might be interested in those new services. In a meeting with the leadership from a small organization in Kyiv,

Ukraine, I found they were thinking mostly of improving their legislative internship program, but I encouraged them to think more broadly to consider how they could improve their government. A whole new set of potential interest groups came to light from this discussion – what would the woman at the next table, the taxi driver, the university student, or the citizen in general want from the organization? The answer was: an organization focused on improving government. The process of stakeholder assessment can significantly expand your universe of potential donors, volunteers, and other supporters – and can lead to increased funding results and program impact. Get everyone involved in thinking about expanding your stakeholders.

R13 WORKSHEET: STAKEHOLDER ASSESSMENT
– Comprehensive format

What do our stakeholders (key interest groups) want from us?

Stakeholders are individuals, groups, or entities who are important to achieving our goals.

They give us money, time, advice, work, endorsement, effort, attention, or something else of value. Organizations that do not satisfy the needs of stakeholders are soon out of business!

(Add as many lines for different entities, groups, subgroups, and individuals as you can.)

Participants representing different departments or functions do this best. Add as many lines as needed.

Who are our stakeholders?	What do we get from them?	What do they want from us?	How do we satisfy them?	How do we know?	Other comments

Brainstorm possible long-term results of your work (one hour)

Brainstorming desired long-term results of your work is intended to stretch participants' thinking about what your nonprofit could possibly achieve with the broadest possible benefits to society. This activity builds on the dreams session, but it is more focused and provides background for later work on vision, mission, goals, strategies, and culture.

Based on your awareness from the stakeholder analysis, this is an exercise where you think openly and creatively about the work you could do. Don't let any barriers block your thinking at this point. Take your dreams from earlier in the retreat and make them more tangible. This activity includes taking a look at what your stakeholders want from you and making what you do more important for them. Ensure you are truly having a meaningful impact on society!

- What could you possibly achieve in the world? What benefits would that be to society?
- How could you extend your programs or donor base in completely new ways?
- How much could you help to solve major problems in society?
- What could your work possibly achieve in ten years or fifteen years?
- What could you innovate that others would want to scale up dramatically?
- What breakthrough improvements would capture the attention of government leaders, business executives, opinion leaders, major donors, and others?

Here is an example of a nonprofit's impact on society and benefits to a wide variety of stakeholders: The real results from training health workers in immunization is not creating a team of trained medical workers or even the resulting number of immunizations. The real results are healthy kids, lower national healthcare costs, and a more productive workforce.

What are results? The real results from a fundraising workshop for my clients are not motivated, strategic, and smart fundraisers (outputs). The real results are not even the increased contributions they produce (outcomes). The real results are bigger and better organizations and the increased impact they have on society.

The longer-term results from the work of your organization may not be evident for many years, but understanding what they *could be* can lead to innovative thinking about important new activities and stronger messaging.

An example of this comes from my work with the National Center for Healthy Housing. Initially, this organization worked to identify solutions to the problem of lead paint in housing and resulting brain damage, especially to young children who ingested dust or chips from lead paint. This organization's leaders were looking for a way to communicate the larger significance of their work. When they identified that eliminating the lead paint hazard from housing would, in the long run, mean fewer brain-damaged kids and adults, fewer resulting health problems, fewer emergency room visits, less antisocial behavior, higher educational achievement, greater life satisfaction, and the resulting cost savings in healthcare, social services, and education, they were able to get key opinion leaders and influential decision-makers to assign a higher priority to their work.

As another example, when I first facilitated this activity with WBNA, the neighborhood association in Providence, Rhode Island, we identified really big long-term results we hoped to achieve in different areas of life in the city. This type of thinking attracted more people to our meetings. We found that identifying really big results was an effective way to involve members of the community as well as political leaders, corporate leaders, and others. Within one year, we secured significant funding from foundation, corporate, and city support.

My motto after that was: "Think big to achieve big. Think long-term to get big!" In my work in training and consulting, people often ask me, "How successful was the workshop?" I always say that we won't know for six or twelve months or even for several years. Evaluation of a workshop really can be done only when time has passed and participants report back on what they have achieved as a result of the workshop – and how this has increased the success of their organization's work.

For many years, the International Federation of Red Cross and Red Crescent Societies (IFRC) organized an annual skill-sharing workshop for the top fundraisers from the National Societies around the world. When I joined the Federation as head of organizational development, organizing the fundraising skill-share became one of my responsibilities. The evaluations for past workshops had focused on the workshop itself and did not address the real results of the workshop.

In my invitation to participants for the next session, I made it clear that they would be expected to make new plans for a fundraising project based on the lessons and examples presented – and that they would be evaluated six months after the workshop on what they actually accomplished. By the last afternoon of the three-day session, participants had seen many exciting examples of innovative fundraising strategies and successful steps for organizational development.

At the beginning of that final session, I pointed to a chart on the wall where participants were expected to write their name, the title of their new fundraising project, and the amount they expected to raise. Then I held up tickets to the gala dinner that night and said, "When you enter your name and fundraising project, I'll give you your dinner ticket." Everyone got to work. And everyone got a ticket.

Six months later, we conducted the evaluation – not on the quality of food, accommodations, or presentations at the workshop – but on what each participant had actually accomplished. The final results: About a third of the participants reported success with their project, another third gave reasons why they could not implement the project, and a third did not reply. The first group was excited and proud to share their results, the second group had excuses that were sometimes valid, and the third group included participants who had left their

What are Results?

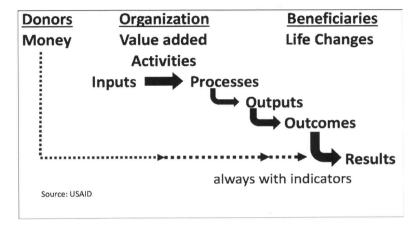

positions or just did not believe we would evaluate them. I was disappointed in the findings, but they were better than not evaluating the actual workshop results. Plus, the process was instructive for many of the participants. In the following years, we continued to focus on improving the long-term results of the fundraising skill-share!

If your planning group is relatively small, you can brainstorm possible long-term results together in a single session. If you have a larger group (more than ten people), this is best done in smaller groups of five to seven people. The task is to produce a list of possible impacts for the benefit of society: breakthrough possibilities and high hopes in short statements with no barriers and no critical comments. Stretch your thinking! Someone captures these ideas for analysis and refinement. Whereas the earlier activity on dreams was about vision, this activity on impacts and results is about mission. Both are important as you move to the next day to tackle actual strategic planning.

R14 WORKSHEET: DESIRED LONG-TERM RESULTS

What are our possible long-term results?

You need to know what results you *ultimately* want to achieve. These long-term impacts are the best possible benefits to society and the best possible value you could create. For each result, list the general term, for example, reduced healthcare costs, increased school graduation rates, increased number of affordable housing units, reduction of the homeless population, decreased violence against women, or the elimination of underserved people in your city. Remember your dreams and what your stakeholders want. Think openly, creatively, and out of the box. Your long-term results should be significant. They should be inspiring. They should ultimately be measurable. They would make your organization famous. (Add as many lines for different entities, groups, subgroups, and individuals as you can.)

What are our possible long-term results? What are the indicators?

1. _____

2. _____

3. _____

+ _____

The exercise on possible long-term results gives the participants meaningful high-level targets for what they want to achieve. It opens the way to higher and broader goals in your plans. Don't worry – these are not yet actual goals for your work. This step is using creativity to expand your thinking about the possibilities you might achieve.

At the end of Day One, you will have a clear understanding of realities and possibilities to guide you in your strategic deliberations in Day Two. The strategic planning in Day Two focuses on creating inspiring and motivating new strategic directions, while the operational level planning in Day Three focuses on realistic objectives and specific steps to take in the short term.

Working groups during and after dinner can address specific issues and report back the next morning. One useful task is for a small team to prepare a PowerPoint synthesis of the outputs from the day's sessions. At the end of the day, you should celebrate your progress with a relaxing reception and dinner.

Questions for implementation

1. What have you achieved thus far in understanding the realities you face? What more do you need to do to assure your planning is grounded in reality?

2. You need to be realistic. How will you use the reality from this session in your next retreat sessions?

3. You need to be creative (new thinking) and innovative (new implementation). How will you use the creativity from this session in your next retreat sessions?

"I want to find my way as the social
entrepreneur I am meant to be!"

"OK. Let's get serious.
Let's decide how we get ahead."

8

Drafting your strategic plan – Day Two

When drafting your strategic plan, newer and smaller organizations should consider a three-year timeframe; larger and more experienced organizations can use a five-year timeframe. Build your plan on the research and creative thinking as well as the discussions, ideas, and insights from Day One of your planning. Be sure to review all the completed research worksheets (R1-R14)!

This chapter will help you arrive at the most important elements of your strategic plan: the ideal world you want to see for those you serve (vision), what you will do to work toward that ideal (mission), your most fundamental beliefs (core values), what you will achieve in the next three or five years (strategic goals), and how you will do it (key strategies). This chapter offers detailed guidance for every step in this process as well as examples and worksheets. Remember to download the detailed worksheets for use by all participants from www.NGOFutures.com.

As you get ready, refer again to the conclusions you made in Appendix 1 (What needs to be done in your strategic plan?) and Appendix 2 (Considerations to prepare for your strategic planning). In addition to the *planning worksheets* in this chapter (P1-P13), the website has four more worksheets on the topics of benefits, revenues, structure, and next steps (P14-P17).

Keep in mind that you should address the topics in this order: vision, mission, and values as the most important elements of your organization. Next, you should conduct a detailed SWOT analysis (strengths, weaknesses, opportunities, threats) based on your research and creative thinking as well as your newly defined vision, mission, and values. This information provides essential input to identify the critical issues you must address to be successful.

Identifying the critical issues leads logically to identifying your strategic goals – what you must do to address the critical issues. For example, if a critical problem is lack of developed fundraising capacity, then quite obviously the strategic goal is to develop fundraising capacity. Note that a goal can relate to more than one department or function; for example, other departments have important responsibilities to support fundraising.

Now you are able to address other important strategic issues – who you are (positioning) and why people should trust you (trustworthiness). In many organizations, the group breaks into two teams to simultaneously address these two issues and report back to the full group for discussion and endorsement. Once the strategic directions are clear, you can also address organization culture (how you work). Your organization needs to function smoothly and be focused on achieving results – this is what the new, desired organization culture describes. For smaller and mid-size organizations, this can take place during the retreat with everyone in attendance. For larger organizations, this discussion should be held after the retreat to involve all staff members. Part IV contains in-depth guidance to explore core values and create your new, desired culture.

The following twelve steps offer detailed advice, examples, and worksheets to create your strategic plan. This should be a cooperative and results-oriented day. In fact, it is pivotal! As a reminder, the template agenda for a strategic planning retreat (Appendix 3) offers a helpful, high-level view of Day Two's progression.

Even a nonprofit with good strategic planning experience will benefit from addressing each of the following steps. Although a given step may require less time, consideration will help you ensure everything is up to date, and the process will confirm staff involvement and commitment.

Step 1: Review what you accomplished in Day One and what to do next (half an hour)

Open the session with a quick synthesis of the outputs from the previous sessions with PowerPoint slides or flip charts (edited the evening before). Those first steps were all intended to get everyone to think deeply about your organization's current reality and to open your minds creatively to the most important possibilities of what your work might accomplish.

In the review, you should highlight the most important conclusions from the previous sessions about reality (history, lessons learned, survey findings, competitor assessment, donor assessment, department director analysis, interviews, planning process, landscape), and possibility (dreams, stakeholder assessments, long-term results). Everyone should be guided throughout the planning by both the reality in which you are working and the possibilities you could realize if you stretch and push yourselves. The following worksheet might be helpful.

P1 WORKSHEET: KEY ISSUES WE MUST ADDRESS

1. How can we plan better (responsibilities)?
2. What do we need to consider in our programs (results)?
3. What do we need to consider in our fundraising and marketing (growth)?

4. What do we need to consider in finance and administration (efficiency)?

5. What do we need to consider in our trustworthiness and positioning (image)?

6. What about promotion, volunteers, education, and advocacy (outreach)?

7. What about issues in culture, staffing, and teamwork (behavior)?

8. What about issues in our governance, leadership, and management (top-level issues)?

9. How else can we organize ourselves to produce better results (impact)?

10. What other issues need to be addressed (no topic off limits)?

Keep in mind the key attributes and essential responsibilities of nonprofit organizations. You may want to share these two charts as you address vision, mission, and values. (The PowerPoint slides I use are also available on my website for free download.)

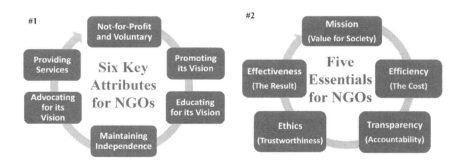

Step 2: Define your vision – What you *ideally* want to see in the world (one hour or longer)

Now you are ready to make one of the most important decisions in your planning process – to determine or revise your vision. The vision is your statement of the ideal world you would like to see in the long run for your program and beneficiaries, based on your own dreams and possible long-term results. It is a utopian statement. For example, the vision for Save the Children includes the concept that all children are healthy, educated, well treated, live in healthy homes, and are optimistic about their future. What I identified for my work as a consultant is a world in which nonprofits are highly effective and efficient, trusted and accountable, producing great results, and society supports them fully.

Examples of short vision statements

1. The National Center for Healthy Housing: "Healthy housing for all"
2. Ukrainian Down Syndrome Organization: "Kids with Downs are healthy, educated, able to work, and maybe find love in their lives"
3. West Broadway Neighborhood Association: "The best neighborhood in the city"
4. GreeningRozzie: "A green community"
5. NYC Kids Project: "A tolerant world"
6. Ken Phillips: "Society is civil"

What is your organization's vision for the ideal world in your field of activity? To process this, it is best to have several small groups of four to seven people working together to draft a phrase that describes the vision that inspires and excites them (or review and improve your current vision statement). Then the groups share their different drafts, and everyone decides on the best synthesis of ideas to produce a single phrase or sentence that excites and motivates all of you. I particularly like a vision that *inspires* others to get involved.

A vision should be clear, short, memorable, and inspiring – that is, visionary. Your vision should attract potential stakeholders and inspire everyone to be interested in your work.

What is your team's vision for the organization? A good vision satisfies these questions:

- Is your vision visionary?
- Does it create value for society?
- Is it clear, short, and memorable?
- Does it reflect your group's dreams for the world?
- Will it inspire stakeholders? Donors? Participants? Staff? Others?

P2 WORKSHEET: VISION

What is the vision of our organization?

What is the ideal world we see for those we serve? The organization's vision is a description of the ultimate perfection of what could be – a utopia. It is what we believe the world should be. It is a short and memorable statement.

Our vision is:

Take the time you need, as this is one of the most important parts of your strategic directions. Good leadership and facilitation help this process. When you get it right from the small group work and full group discussions, there will be a sigh of relief and a whoop of excitement!

Step 3: Define your mission – What you *do* to work toward your vision (one hour or longer)

On the basis of your vision, you can now draft or update your mission – what you do to help achieve your vision. Your mission describes whom you serve, what you do, and how you do that. It should be a short statement people can remember, follow, and communicate to others. And, especially, be sure it is based on reality, since a good mission has a reasonable chance of success. A mission based on wishful thinking or just on the sole view of one person (perhaps the founder, CEO, or a key stakeholder) is a mission heading toward failure.

Here are a few example mission statements:

- The mission of Save the Children is to provide funding and technical assistance to families and communities in health, education, family support, housing, and income-producing activities to assure their children's futures.

- The mission of GreeningRozzie is to make Roslindale, Massachusetts, a greener, cleaner, and more cohesive community by working together to promote and implement grassroots projects and activities.

- The mission of NYC Kids Project is to provide educational programs in schools and other locations to teach tolerance and understanding.

- The mission for my consulting business is to provide knowledge, tools, and motivation to nonprofit executives, so they can lead, manage, and build capacity in their organizations to be effective and efficient, trusted and accountable, and produce increased revenues and great results to make this a better world. (Here is my short version: Provide valued support to NGOs to transform themselves to be stronger and better in their work to make a better world.)

- The mission of InterAction is "a convener, thought leader, and voice for NGOs working to eliminate extreme poverty, strengthen human rights and citizen participation, safeguard a sustainable planet, promote peace, and ensure dignity for all people."

Peter Drucker, one of the most strategic organizational experts, posed fundamental questions every organization must ask itself.

His questions combine vision and mission, stakeholder expectations, and organization planning. It is worth the time to think deeply about the five issues Drucker identifies:

- What is your mission?
- Who is your customer?
- What does the customer value?
- What is your plan?
- What are your results?

Your mission statement should be short, memorable, and empowering. I particularly like an empowering mission that gives staff, volunteers, donors, participants, and others the power and confidence to achieve the inspiring vision.

What is the mission for your organization? A good mission satisfies these questions:

- Is it focused on contribution to the world?
- Does it address the needs of participants?
- Does it achieve worthwhile purposes?
- Is it empowering for stakeholders? Donors? Participants? Staff? Others?
- Does it create a collective "Yes!"?

P3 WORKSHEET: MISSION

What is the mission of our organization?

What do we actually do to achieve our vision? A good mission statement describes whom we serve, what needs we meet, and how we help. It reflects, supports, and contributes to our organization's vision. It is broad enough to allow flexibility yet provides focus. It is clear and brief enough to remember and serve as a rallying point. What do we do? Whom do we serve? How do we help? It is a short and memorable statement.

Our mission is:

Step 4: Define or clarify the core values that guide everything you do (one hour or longer)

A nonprofit organization, as you know, raises money from one set of stakeholders to provide benefits to another set of stakeholders. This is completely different from the business model of the corporate world. With corporations, the consumer generally purchases a product or service to benefit himself or herself and pays an agreed amount to the seller. You know what you get.

Nonprofits, on the other hand, ask donors to contribute funds, time, or other resources to benefit other people or the larger community. Since the world of nonprofits is built on *voluntary* support, the matter of trust is paramount. To be trustworthy, an organization must have a set of core values that guide and shape everything it does. As I emphasized earlier, core values are fundamental and non-negotiable. They guide *everything* you do. Values are most effective when they are relatively few in number and stated in a brief and memorable format.

The core values of a major healthcare organization, as an example, are respect, integrity, compassion, and excellence. The core values of my high school are cooperation, humility, empathy, humor, connectedness, independence of mind, and awareness of diverse perspectives. Core values are important and differ from one organization to another. Part IV covers core values and organization culture in more detail. If you have any question about your core values, you will benefit from that guidance.

P4 WORKSHEET: CORE VALUES - Short format

What are our core values?

Core values are the beliefs, norms, and ideas that shape how an organization carries out its mission. They influence activities within the organization and identify the basis of how we treat staff, volunteers, donors, participants, and others. Core values guide us in all we do. State them in just a few words or brief memorable phrases. Make them strong core values.

Our core values are:

1.

2.

3.

+

These three statements – vision, mission, and values – are the three most important components in your strategic plan and in your work. They should fit together and reinforce each other. All three should be strong statements that flow over into your work and communications.

Step 5: Assess strengths and weaknesses + opportunities and threats (one to two hours)

Now that you have your vision, mission, and values statements, it is time to analyze your nonprofit's strengths and weaknesses and your opportunities and threats (SWOT) to carry out your organization's work. You should be motivated by the dreams and results sessions, informed by what donors and other stakeholders want, and guided by lessons learned, findings from surveys, and other reports and recommendations.

Mixed groups of staff from different departments are best for this exercise to avoid in-grown or defensive perspectives. The involvement of some volunteers and, if possible, program participants or representatives will also help to produce valid assessments of internal factors (your strengths and weaknesses) and external factors (your opportunities and threats). And it is smart to consult with leading board members to make sure you are aware of any views they may have.

When conducting your SWOT analysis, everyone must be open and honest about your organization's internal strengths and weaknesses. You must not ignore external threats or opportunities. Planning that is based on inaccurate statements or avoidance of problems is like a house built on sand or even quicksand.

In my work with nonprofits, people often raise external issues as their biggest barriers. They cite a recession or economic malaise, worry about the future, government cutbacks, wealth concentrated in just a few families, absence of a national culture of giving, severe competition among NGOs, and the like. These are serious concerns, but you should not think about them or use them as excuses.

The SWOT analysis is one of the most important sessions leading to good strategic planning. This activity gets you to focus on what you can do and what you must do.

The barriers you should consider are the ones you can do something about. The many internal examples include: not making your case appealing, being afraid to ask for support, just hoping projects will work, not being trusted, top executives and board members not being involved in fundraising, internal conflicts, programs without clear results, poor planning, disagreements between program and fundraising, not making plans work, lack of a fundraising culture, and other internal weaknesses.

Some external problems such as poor laws for nonprofits or the lack of a tradition of philanthropy in your country are real issues that you can best address by joining with other nonprofit organizations for advocacy and lobbying action.

P5 WORKSHEET: SWOT ANALYSIS

What are our internal strengths and weaknesses?
What are our external opportunities and threats?

The situation assessment is an honest, thoughtful analysis of the reality in which we work.

- How do we see the situation?
- What's good? What's not? Be candid!
- What are the most important trends? Politics, economics, culture, technology?

- What do we do best? Worst?
- What is our competition doing?

The SWOT captures all the assessments and analyses we have done. (Add lines as needed.)

Our major internal strengths are:	Our major internal weaknesses are:
+	–
+	–
+	–
Our key outside opportunities are:	**Our key outside threats are:**
+	–
+	–
+	–

Once you have completed this assessment, the group should look at what you have identified in each of the four areas of the SWOT analysis. The key challenge here is using your SWOT findings to identify ways to break new ground. You can achieve real breakthroughs in organizational development and growth if you focus on how to:

- Strengthen your strengths
- Overcome your weaknesses
- Take advantage of opportunities
- Turn threats into opportunities

Your SWOT analysis provides important inputs into your strategic goals and key strategies and, later, your operational plans. Strengthening strengths and overcoming weaknesses are obvious steps to become a stronger organization. Capitalizing on opportunities, turning weaknesses into strengths, and transforming threats into opportunities are challenges to see things in new ways and develop new strategies. An optimistic and positive attitude about all these issues is the smart approach. It is an energizing experience for staff to see top management openly address these issues.

Step 6: Identify the critical issues you *must* solve (one hour or more)

Now it is time for the planning group to review and consider everything from the research you have heard, the analysis you have done, and the results you want achieve, along with the assessment of your capabilities. Use all of this as input to determine the most critical issues you must solve in order to succeed. You can do this in small groups working to extract, synthesize, and summarize the most important issues from all the preceding steps. As facilitator, I find it is extremely useful if I walk around and make sure the groups are really focusing on the big issues.

Critical issues usually relate to programs and services, fundraising and awareness, finance and internal operations, and organizational strengthening and innovation. Expansion, growth, staff competencies, culture, and board development are often on the list. A critical issue for most organizations, for example, is how can you compete with larger, more powerful nonprofits.

When identifying the critical issues you must solve, the challenge is to refine the list of issues by eliminating, combining, and broadening topics until there is a reasonable number of the most important broad issues. Aim for a list of about five to seven issues. (A list of three or four issues is probably insufficient, and a list of eight or nine issues is overwhelming.) A critical issue can have a number of sub-issues, which are part of the bigger issue but are addressed by different departments or teams in the organization. These sub-issues are then addressed in the functional areas' operational plans with separate objectives that, together, address and solve the larger critical issue.

Critical issues for your organization are:

- Issues that flow directly from your research, creativity, and analysis
- Issues that significantly impact your ability to perform
- Issues on which you have influence or control
- Issues you must solve in order to survive and thrive
- Issues that grow into serious problems if you fail to solve them

Whereas the sessions on dreams and long-term results were in the appreciative inquiry mode of unrestrained creativity, the steps to identify critical issues and strategic goals are practical, hard-nosed, and solutions-oriented. Your vision, dreams, and long-term results get you to look at the mountaintop, while the research, mission, SWOT, and critical issues get you to look at the mountain side with the goal of getting to the top.

This discussion gets everyone to look objectively at problems and how to fix them. To do this well, participants in a planning group should focus on realistic but confident solution thinking. In *problem thinking*, people talk about problems, blame, and causes. In *solution thinking*, people talk about the same problems but focus on results, change, and options to achieve them.

Problem thinkers focus on the past, while solution thinkers focus on the future. Responses to new ideas by problem thinkers are: "It won't work" or "yes, but ..." while solution thinkers respond with enthusiasm, more brainstorming, and more options. Problem thinkers are unable to move past the problem, while solution thinkers find the positive and endorse needed changes to get things done.

Problem thinkers are negative and frustrated by problems, but solution thinkers are positive and energized to solve problems!

Another key consideration is to focus on identifying the big issues, not small ones that can be readily resolved. Even worse is picking the big problems that urgently do need to be solved but then selecting ineffective or counterproductive solutions. This is a disaster in planning, because you'll only make the situation worse. Clearly, you need to identify the big, important, critical issues to address, so you can later create the right solutions, plans, and strategies that will effectively solve the problems.

After the small groups have done their work to extract, synthesize, and summarize the most important challenges, bring the entire group back together for feedback. I find it keeps interest to have each group report on one critical issue at a time and go around the room to collect what could be a fairly long list of issues. Very often groups will suggest similar issues or components of a larger issue. The facilitator captures similar issues together on the flip chart and (with assent from the group) combines and synthesizes issues into more compact statements of the critical issues. If different groups suggest the same issue, then you simply put a big checkmark next to the issue already written on the flip chart. Some issues are best addressed in another forum, and these are put in a "parking lot" for later.

The target here is to combine and synthesize to end up with a reasonable number of high-level critical issues the organization must address. Once you identify the most important critical issues, you are on your way to a great strategic plan.

P6 WORKSHEET: CRITICAL ISSUES

What critical issues do we have to solve?

Critical issues are the five to seven biggest issues we have to solve. Identifying critical issues flows directly from the analysis about our organization, our situation, and our stakeholders. Without identifying and solving these issues, we will not succeed. Critical issues are the issues we must address to survive and perform well.

- Each critical issue is stated in a few words, not a full sentence.
- There will be serious problems if we fail to address these critical issues.
- They are the major issues to focus on for the next few years.
- They are issues we can influence or control.
- For every threat there is an opportunity! For every weakness there is a solution!

Our critical issues are:

1.

2.

3.

4.

5.

+

Step 7: Identify the strategic goals for your organization (half an hour)

Based on the critical issues listed above, you can identify the five to seven strategic goals for your organization for the coming few years. Goals build on your dreams and desired long-term results and are stretching but achievable within a reasonable period.

Strategic goals state where you want to be at the end of the time period selected.

- Goals respond directly to the critical issues you just identified.
- They are general destinations on the way toward your vision.
- Goals work together to achieve progress in your overall mission as you move forward.
- They represent significant changes and are realistic and stretching.
- Each goal has a single focus with a single key result.
- Each goal specifies what you will achieve, not the how or why.
- Each goal is written as a completed action stating where you will be at the end of the period.

There are usually goals for programs and services, fundraising and public relations, finance and administration, and organizational strengthening. They could also include monitoring and evaluation, staff training and learning systems, advocacy and lobbying, board strengthening and more.

Identifying the goals can be a surprisingly quick process, since you can effectively turn the critical issues into achievements. As an example, perhaps your smaller nonprofit identified this critical issue: "Competing with similar but larger nonprofits for mindshare, donors, and funds is an ever-growing problem. If we cannot overcome this threat, we will fail." Therefore, the goal for competing with larger organizations is: "We align with similar small NGOs that share, learn, and grow together." (Here's the rationale: Ten small NGOs more than equal an NGO ten times larger thanks to the group's dispersed creativity, specialization, strategy, teamwork, sharing, and cooperation. As a result of working in cooperation, NGOs grow stronger, increase their exposure and reputation, grow their donor base, and increase funds.)

P7 WORKSHEET: STRATEGIC GOALS

What are our strategic goals?

Strategic goals state where we want to be at the end of the planning period. They are important goals for service delivery, fundraising, and other capacity building for three to five years. Strategic goals are written as accomplishments with a single result and a single focus for each. Our strategic goals are the basis for our operational plans.

- Direct responses to identified critical issues
- General destinations on our mission
- Responses to stakeholder expectations
- What we must have achieved to succeed
- Realistic, stretching, and significant
- Statements of what (not how or why)

Our strategic goals are:

1.

2.

3.

4.

5.

+

Step 8: Identify key strategies that will define *how* you move forward (several hours)

Planning now moves to strategies. Strategies are the roadmap for your work. Strategies indicate *how* you will move forward and how you will achieve the results you desire. They are important components of your strategic plan and are usually the hardest to work through. Each strategy has significant implications for formulating tactical objectives, specific activities, progress indicators, required personnel, budgets, and so forth. The key strategies you choose will guide you in all of your decision-making and have a major impact on the objectives, activities, personnel, and resources you identify in your operational plans.

When I facilitate a planning process, I address the topic of key strategies when participants have a clear view of where they are heading, based on the direction provided by their new (or updated) vision, mission, and values statements along with the goals they have identified. When you address key strategies with your group, it is important to look back at these elements. The research findings especially related to program and funding and the statements for vision, mission, values, and goals often lead to obvious conclusions about the appropriate new key strategies. Note: If the group identifies a new unexpected, innovative, or disruptive strategy, then you may need to revise the goals to assure your strategic goals and key strategies are in perfect alignment.

At this point in your planning process, I suggest you focus first on identifying and developing just the single most important strategy for the organization. This may be the core organizational strategy or the core program strategy. Organizational strategies, for example, could be a focus on advocacy (such as Greenpeace), a focus on grant making with expertise in selecting and monitoring grantees (such as the Civil

Society Development Foundation in Romania), a focus to expand your impact by identifying and supporting partner organizations (such as the International Youth Foundation), or a focus to expand the population you serve to everyone in the community rather than one segment (such as the West Broadway Neighborhood Association). Notice that strategy statements are brief (supporting details are always included in the operational plans).

Another organization-wide strategy is a strategy to drive operational efficiency and cost savings. We did this at Foster Parents Plan with a version of Total Quality Management led by staff teams identifying ways to reduce paper flow and other inefficiencies. This produced substantial savings in time and costs.

Other possible program strategies are to launch an innovative program experiment, implement a uniquely efficient program with larger than usual results, demonstrate why you have the best program in a particular category, secure independent evaluation that proves superior results, and promote your program to major grant-makers and government for large scale expansion and replication. Keep in mind, however, that strategy must be supported with sufficient research, knowledge, and budget. With strategy, we are not dealing in dreams; we are focused on realties and *how* to progress.

Here are examples of strategies for two nonprofit organizations:

- As mentioned earlier in this book, the key organizational strategy at Foster Parents Plan was increasing the fundraising effort to grow income. This effort led to a tripling of the income and number of donors with substantial increases in funding for program activities.

- At Save the Children, the key strategy was a new community-based integrated development program that helped families and their children – and was appealing to donors along with new fundraising diversification, branding, and public awareness.

It is also useful to have strategies for different functions and departments. When I facilitate three-day retreats, I ask the different departments to develop their own strategies for their respective functions and report back to the full group. Rather than exploring the many important strategies for fundraising and marketing here, I will share this in my next book: *25 Proven Strategies for Fundraising Success: How to win the love and support of donors.*

P8 WORKSHEET: ORGANIZATION STRATEGY
– Short format

What is our key organization strategy?

A strategy is a clear and logical explanation of how we will progress (what path, what means). Strategy is the roadmap to arrive at our goals, crafted to fit the special situation of the organization and its stakeholders. Identifying strategies requires creativity and insight. Strategy is the basis for our decisions, setting objectives and priorities, and allocating resources.

Our key organization strategy is:

Step 9: Define your positioning: *Who* you are and how you present yourself (two hours)

You have a vision of the world, a mission of your work, your strategic goals, and your key strategy. But who are you? It is important for your organization to define itself clearly and simply. In this way, you position yourself in the field of your activity for program and in the marketplace for funding. In this step, your interviews, surveys, and assessments of donors and competitors are particularly important. How well do your stakeholders know your nonprofit? What appeals to them about your organization? How do you differentiate yourself from your key competitors? What is unique and special about you?

This step (defining your positioning) – along with the next two steps on trustworthiness and organization culture – are specific strategy statements every organization must have. These three statements define how you will work internally to achieve the goals and objectives in your plans. In my experience, if you do not have clear statements for all three of these, you will face problems and shortfalls.

When it comes to positioning, we know from advertising studies that when people shop they tend to respond to products whose names they know and whose image or reputation they like. It is the same for donors, since they see numerous opportunities from different organizations to contribute. *This is the awareness factor.*

In your positioning, it is also advantageous to show how you are unique. For nonprofits, this can translate into having a strong donor base (for example, all the parents of children with Down syndrome), an image that dominates (for example, a famous person's name or prestigious people on the board or honorary board), or a uniquely effective program approach (for example, the best results for kids or the cure for a disease). *This is the uniqueness factor.*

Your strategic positioning includes your organization's name and logo, a brief description of who you are, and a slogan (or tagline). Together, these communicate to your various publics your uniqueness and importance.

I hope your nonprofit's name itself communicates who you are and what you do. If it doesn't, your communications start off with a deficit. A well-known organization such as UNICEF can use initials, because it is so widely known due to its worldwide activities and huge promotion budget. But few organizations have these business benefits. So please, no initials! *This is the image factor.*

One of my first strategic plans, as mentioned earlier, was when I was director of the fundraising department at Save the Children in the United States some fifty years ago. I created a new plan for four reasons:

- Get better fundraising results.
- Identify and use a strong brand in our marketing and public relations.
- Align the management team, so they would do more in their departments to support fundraising.
- Secure overall agreement from the executive director on plans, so I would spend less time with him day-to-day and on weekends.

At that time, the nonprofit was using "SCF" and "the Federation" in its reports, communications, and advertising – short for Save the Children Federation, the formal name of the organization. The logo was a geometric box with a tiny child figure. When I joined the organization, it was relatively unknown and was raising only $3 million annually in the U.S. As part of our planning process, we developed an innovative and more effective program strategy to help children by providing financial assistance and technical support to entire communities, so the communities could help themselves through a variety of activities focused on child, family, and community development. The result was greater impact on children and their families and a stronger appeal to more varied donors.

The board of directors of the organization thought we should change the name from Save the Children to Community Development Foundation. At first, I was the lone voice who said that Save the Children was a uniquely attractive name and brand. Eventually the board and executive director agreed. In the new strategic fundraising plan, we rolled out the new program approach under the brand Save the Children, which is a memorable and appealing name, states the powerful mission of the organization, and simultaneously presents a compelling call to action. Our new logo presented a child figure with raised arms, and our slogan was "Saving children through family and community development." Now it is one of the best known nonprofits in the U.S. and raised $881 million in 2018. Brand matters!

One way of looking at positioning is to think about identity (who you are) and image (who people think you are). You should strive to have your identity and image mirror each other, so there will be authenticity in your positioning.

Logo matters, too! A good logo immediately and visually communicates who you are and what you do. As an example, the UNICEF logo has evolved over 70 years to be an inspiring image of a mother lifting up a child within a wreath of peace, with a tagline of "Saving Lives, Building Futures."

Developing the strategic positioning statement for your organization can be done in a group process in Day Two of your strategic planning retreat or addressed by a small taskforce of experts and strategic thinkers, based on your new strategic directions. The taskforce would work separately and report back to the full planning group.

P9 WORKSHEET: STRATEGIC POSITIONING

What is our desired image or strategic positioning (unique value added)?

Our strategic positioning shows who we are and how we are attractive to stakeholders. Donors pay us to perform a service. They could give their funds to another nonprofit or business. We are in competition with other organizations for awareness and funds, and the competition is severe. We want to appeal to donors with something special and add more value to a donor's gift than their other expenditures could. We need to think of our uniqueness, the value of our work, and how we communicate these points. This is our strategic positioning and brand, which together form our image.

Our name is:
Our logo is:
Our positioning or identity is:
Our slogan or tagline is:

Step 10: Draft a credibility statement showing why people can *trust* you (two hours)

Based on your values and key strategies, you should also draft a credibility statement, which states how you demonstrate your values and warrant the trust of donors. Expectations of stakeholders – whether they are donors, participants, staff, partners, officials, or others – are that your nonprofit is effective, efficient, trustworthy, and accountable.

A credibility statement can include, as a minimum, publishing a comprehensive annual report, externally audited financial statements, a code of ethics with no conflicts of interests, and other indicators of trustworthy behavior. Other key elements to deserve trust include:

- Truthful fundraising appeals
- Use of funds according to donor expectations
- Transparency and accountability to donors and others
- Sound financial management and accurate financial reports
- Active, informed, and independent board members
- Adherence to best practices in all aspects of work
- Complete, accurate, and timely program reports
- Measured program effectiveness

The organization's leadership should also work to build a culture of trustworthiness and accountability through internal systems:

- Set a personal example by leadership
- Make this part of how you do your work
- Make it a way of living in the organization
- Conduct an audit of accountability
- Reinforce ethics in recruitment, orientation, and training
- Maintain a confidential suggestion box or feedback system
- Have a recognition and reward system
- Offer a whistle-blower channel
- Communicate all this externally

After developing your values and credibility statements, you should test them on randomly selected people in your community – the person next to you on the bus, your family members, the people at the next table in the restaurant, and the taxi driver – or in a more formal research project. Listen to them carefully and understand what you need to do and say to be credible. Make updates and revisions as you learn more and confirm your statement.

Developing the credibility statement can be done in the group process or by a small taskforce of experts and strategic thinkers who meet separately and report their conclusions to the planning group, based on your new strategic directions.

P10 WORKSHEET: CREDIBILITY OR TRUSTWORTHINESS

What is our credibility statement to convince stakeholders they can *trust* us?

Why should anyone trust us? Stakeholders need to trust us to give us their money, time, work, advice, and other forms of support. What are the key elements of our trustworthiness? What about our history, results, integrity, management, governance, finances, audits, accountability, diversity, transparency, reporting, endorsements, assurances, practices, donor service, and code of ethics? We need a credibility statement to demonstrate we are trustworthy.

A credibility statement can include, as a minimum, developing and publishing a comprehensive annual report, externally audited financial statements, a code of ethics with no conflicts of interests, and other indicators of trustworthy behavior.

We state the following as our commitment to accountability and trustworthiness:

1.

2.

3.

+

Step 11: Identify your organization culture and how you should *behave* (several hours)

Culture builds on the organization's core values. Culture is how you behave and work together. A clear statement of your organization culture guides the behavior of everyone involved in the organization's work and also communicates to potential donors how the organization behaves.

One of the presentations I frequently give to nonprofits and NGOs worldwide is "Organization Culture: Is it Oil or Sand in your Plans?" I have seen that the wrong kind of culture can completely undercut or sabotage even the best strategic and operational plans.

Every organization should assess its current culture including, as one workshop participant said, "the good, the bad, and the ugly." Honesty is important here, and honesty is best facilitated in small groups to accurately identify the current culture and then draft a new, desired culture that fully supports the new strategic goals. Then the same small groups should identify what everyone in the organization can do to reinforce the new, desired culture.

I recommend that all staff participate in identifying attributes of the current culture and the new, desired culture. This can be done at the end of Day Two of the strategic planning retreat for many organizations or shortly after the planning retreat for large organizations.

You will find a more detailed discussion for strengthening your values and creating your new, desired culture with step-by-step guidance in Part IV. I encourage you to use the more thorough guidance and worksheets in Part IV for the best result.

P11 WORKSHEET: ORGANIZATION CULTURE – short format

What is our desired organization culture to support our plans?

Culture is the glue that binds people together and gives us a way of behaving and working together. Organization culture unifies vision, mission, values, and people.

- What behaviors currently exist?
- How should these change?
- What is desired for fundraising?

What is our desired organization culture?

Our new, desired culture is:

1.

2.

3.

+

Our plan to reinforce the new culture is:

Step 12: Review the coherence of your strategic plan and set the framework for a review

Now, at the end of Day Two of your strategic planning retreat, you should have a coherent, well-integrated, and overarching statement of strategic directions for your future based on solid research, critical analysis, optimism, realistic thinking, and hard work. At the end of your drafting sessions, you should review the results of your previous steps to make sure all statements support and reinforce each other.

Be sure to make adjustments as needed. Later, an editing team can fine-tune the document.

Although you developed these elements in a different sequence in the planning process, they form a unity of your strategic directions:

- Vision and mission
- Values and culture
- Goals and strategies
- Image and trustworthiness

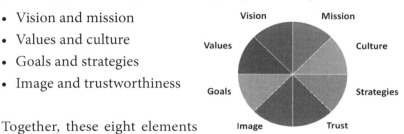

Together, these eight elements constitute your new strategic directions and should form a perfect unity for your organization. When this is the case, you have completed a good planning process with strategic elements that fit neatly together. Once approved, the strategic plan guides all further planning, budgeting, implementing, learning, and development for the organization. A well-managed organization follows the strategic plan enthusiastically and completely.

It is important to make sure the board – which will be asked to approve the final plan – is sufficiently informed, involved, and represented during the planning in order to avoid unexpected criticism or even rejection of the drafted plan. I have seen cases where the executive director has been shocked by a board's refusal to adopt the strategic plan. Steps need to be taken to avoid this serious disruption in planning.

Examples of three organizations' strategic plans

For many people, the concept of developing a strategic plan may seem hefty and burdensome. However, keep in mind that strategic plans can be surprisingly brief and to the point. To that end, I have included four model strategic plans. The first is a small nonprofit that needed to "restart" in New York City. As an informal organization, the NYC Kids Project was funded for many years through government grants until this funding was suddenly terminated. The project uses puppets to teach kids in schools about being tolerant of kids who may be different with various disabilities. Its program was excellent; its new challenges were structure, organization, and funding. When the leaders found themselves with no funding, I helped them envision the new organization and develop the new strategic plan.

The strategic plan of NYC Kids Project

Image: We are the NYC Kids Project. We are an experienced social justice organization working through arts and education to change the world, one child at a time. We create inclusive and safe spaces where children can be heard and where they are encouraged to ask questions and share their stories. Our slogan is: "Listen to them."

Vision: Our vision is an integrated, compassionate, and accessible society where all people are valued, accepted for who they are, and need not fear judgment as each person brings a unique value to the world.

Mission: Using disabilities as a springboard, our mission is to educate and empower the public through the art of theater and puppetry to dispel stereotypes and embrace the commonality of all people.

Values: Fairness and justice, respect and inclusiveness, empathy and compassion, empowerment

Culture: Playfulness and laughter, creativity and curiosity, active learning, trustworthiness and honesty, open mindedness

Critical issue: Lack of resources

Goals: 1) Continue our programs and 2) Generate needed resources

Key strategy: Focus on fundraising and board development

The second example is from a successful nonprofit in Colombia, which provides comprehensive support in communities. We developed this NGO's strategic plan in a three-day retreat following extensive research. The priority was on developing new sources of funding.

The strategic plan of a large nonprofit working in Colombia

Our vision: We work for a world in which all people can live with dignity, integrity, and freedom.

Our mission: We facilitate comprehensive development and upgrading the quality of life of people living in poverty and vulnerability in Colombia, contributing to economic and community development through a transformative approach based on the principles of the Christian faith, empowerment, and sustainability.

Our values:

1. We believe in the intrinsic value of the human being, created in the image and likeness of God.
2. We believe in the five principles of stewardship, compassion, interdependence, love, and identity and the three values of dignity, integrity, and freedom.
3. That people matter.

Our culture: An organization that learns, is competitive externally, and is results oriented. We are Participatory, Respectful, Transparent, Cooperative, Punctual, and Innovative.

Our goals:
1. Strengthen our image and marketing capacity
2. Strengthen and validate our model of community and economic development
3. Develop our skills and leadership
4. Be an innovative organization that learns
5. Strengthen our capacity to be competitive and effective in every environment and sector

The third example is from PLAN International. We formed a multi-country strategic planning committee, which developed the plans in 1992. The organization has certainly developed further since this strategic planning process decades ago, but the plan illustrates important components of a strategic plan.

PLAN International strategic directions

Identity: PLAN International is an international humanitarian, child-focused, development organization, without religious, political, or governmental affiliation. Child sponsorship is the basic foundation of the organization.

Vision: PLAN's vision is of a world in which all children realize their full potential in societies which respect people's rights and dignity.

Mission: PLAN International strives to achieve lasting improvements in the quality of life of deprived children in developing

countries through a process that unites people across cultures
and adds meaning and value to their lives by:

- Enabling deprived children, their families, and their
  communities to meet their basic needs and to increase
  their ability to participate in and benefit from their societies;
- Fostering relationships to increase understanding in unity
  among people of different cultures and countries;
- Promoting the rights and interests of the world's children.

Commitment to quality: PLAN is committed to achieving
excellence in meeting the needs of the people it serves through
the creation and maintenance of an enabling management
environment centered on a process of continuous improvement,
measurement, and systematic support involving all levels of the
organization.

From the above examples, you see that plans are different for
different organizations. It is up to you and your planning participants
to determine the appropriate content and format for your plans.

You can find the most current strategic statements by these
organizations and others on their websites.

Questions for implementation

1. This chapter presents detailed steps for use in Day Two of your strategic planning. What do you need to do to bring your team up to speed to prepare for the planning process?

2. Have you completed the answers in Appendix 1 (What needs to be done in your strategic plan?) and reviewed Appendix 2 (Considerations to prepare for your strategic planning)? What more do you need to do to prepare for a successful Day Two at your retreat?

3. Have you reviewed the detailed worksheets and other tools from www.NGOFutures.com and shared them with the planning participants?

4. Are you confident you can lead a successful process for your new strategic plan?

"I love this process!"

"We're making real progress in getting consensus on key issues."

9

Drafting your operational plans – Day Three

Now that you have developed a brief, targeted strategic plan and you have clear strategic directions for your organization, you can now develop specific operational plans for implementation.

Whether you are a nonprofit or community association, this section offers guidance to develop your operational plans for the coming year. The operational plan for each functional group (such as fundraising, program, or finance/administration) defines what people will do week-to-week and month-to-month to achieve the agreed objectives in the given timeframe. Operational plans are best drafted by the people who will be responsible for implementing them. This ensures they bring their expertise and knowledge to the process. And their commitment!

It is important to note that smaller and mid-size organizations may be able to complete these plans in Day Three of the strategic planning retreat, while larger organizations will need additional time to involve the full staff in the process. A community organization can complete the strategic and operational planning in a full-day retreat or in several evenings of group work.

Operational planning follows the strategic plan to "operationalize" the strategic directions

- *Research* + stakeholder assessments + SWOT = What we based our planning on

- *Vision* + dreams + desired long-term results = What we want to achieve at our best

- *Mission* + strategic goals + operational plans = What we do and and what we will achieve

- *Values* + positioning + credibility + culture = Who we are and and how we work

- *Strategies* + program + funding + management = How we will do it

- *Donors* + participants + staff + volunteers = Who will enable us to succeed

- *Objectives* + activities + responsibilities = What we do day to day

---

Operational plans cover the coming year or a shorter period to adjust to your normal fiscal year. In succeeding years, you will develop a new operational plan annually, improving it each time.

Content and format of operational plans – understanding operational plans

Most organizations will plan to achieve growth in their revenues and improvements in their programs, and therefore your new strategic directions should be pointing in this direction. An open, participatory planning process is more likely to produce successful operational plans, because it will involve the participants at all levels in the organization more fully in determining what they will do to achieve agreed objectives. Involvement = Commitment = Achievement!

Operational plans are essential for all levels of an organization. They cascade down from the strategic plan to all levels:

1. The strategic plan and its goals and strategies establish the strategic directions.
2. All operational plans are designed to contribute to achieving agreed goals and objectives.
3. The objectives for departments and major functions are drafted and then agreed.
4. Operational plans include objectives, activities, individual responsibilities, deadlines, indicators, and reporting as well as staffing, budget, and other resources required.
5. Every unit and individual has a clear job description, annual objectives, activities, and responsibilities that support the goals and objectives.
6. Operational plans are approved by supervisors, department heads, and management.
7. Finally, the organization's topline operational plan summarizes key objectives and expected results for all departments and functions.

The operational plans should align with the essentials of nonprofits: Value – your mission or importance to society; Results – your effectiveness or the quality you achieve; Cost – your efficiency or overhead; Trustworthiness – your ethics and behavior; Accountability – your transparency and reporting to constituents.

Operational plans should also align with the *key attributes of nonprofits*: Promoting your socially worthwhile cause; Providing services in some socially important cause for public benefit; Educating and raising awareness of this cause; Advocating to society, business, and government to gain support for the cause; Remaining a private, voluntary, not-for-profit relying on contributions and volunteer time; Preserving your independent voice and status, so you can better achieve your mission.

Effective operational plans implement a management by objective (MBO) approach

1. Set the *objective* of where you want to be
2. Determine the *activities* to get there
3. Establish the *responsibilities and deadlines*
4. Develop *indicators* of progress
5. Set up a *monitoring* system to identify needed changes to achieve the objectives
6. Determine the *cost* in time and money
7. Establish the *reporting* requirements

From my management experience, I know it is productive to set stretching but achievable objectives. All planning guides present the SMART approach to setting objectives – *Specific, Measurable, Actionable, Results-*focused, and *Time*-limited.

> ### Objectives should be SMART+S
> 1. **S**pecific
> 2. **M**easurable
> 3. **A**ctionable
> 4. **R**esults-focused
> 5. **T**ime-limited
> 6. **S**tretching

I agree and add a final "S" to get plans to *Stretch* performance to greater heights. If you set objectives that are normal or low, they will not stimulate enough effort. If you set them too high, they will be discouraging.

Stretching is just the right amount of ambition to be attainable. Plans can, of course, be adjusted during the year.

Operational plans indicate their contribution to mission and goals – this is the reason you exist and every department, team, and individual should fit into this approach. In short, your operational plans start from what you want to achieve and show how to get there.

Each department's plan should follow a management by objective approach, with a focus on achieving clearly defined "stretch" objectives and what to do to achieve them.

End-of-year objectives

Clear objectives are important for managers, board members, donors, and staff to know what you will be doing, what you expect to achieve, and how funds will be used. Here are a few examples of measurable, clearly defined objectives:

- 10 schools constructed
- 100 tons of food delivered
- 500 classes provided with our education program
- 500 parents recruited to membership
- 1,000 children vaccinated
- 10,000 students graduated
- 100,000 policy petitions signed
- $500,000 in donations raised

Internal objectives are also important, for example:

- Fully implement the new IT system
- Complete all personnel evaluations

- Establish the honorary board of directors
- Recruit three new board members

Operational plans must include key progress indicators (KPIs)

All operational plans should have indicators of periodic progress that are clear and measurable. In a plan without indicators (that is, measurements), you will not know what you are achieving, cannot measure progress along the way or make adjustments, and will be unable to hold anyone accountable. Without indicators, progress is like an amoeba that changes shape all the time. Without progress indicators, achievements become a matter of debate and opinion rather than fact.

Periodic key progress indicators are essential for staff in their work and reports, for supervisors in their support and monitoring, and for management in rewarding good results!

Progress indicators in fundraising, for example, could include the number of grant proposals funded, donors renewed, volunteers recruited, and reports submitted each month. Other examples are completion of something important such as:

- Complete the annual audit within two months after the end of the fiscal year.
- Complete the draft annual report by February 28.
- Publish the annual report within three months after the end of the fiscal year.
- Submit all required reports, audits, licenses, and registrations by the due dates.

Indicators can be geared toward monitoring workflow. Here are a few examples:

- Respond to all donor questions within twenty-four hours.
- Submit three proposals to corporations each month.
- Complete the orientation of new board members within one month of their election.
- Identify and contact five potential new major donors each month.
- Respond to every media opportunity within two days.
- Secure all financial reports by the tenth of the following month.
- Close the accounts within twenty days after the end of each month.

Key progress indicators enable the responsible person and supervisor to monitor progress and make needed corrections. As Joanne Rohde, CEO of Axial Exchange, a software company, states, "You have to measure everything, even if you're doing something that seems hard to measure at first…. Every two weeks, we have a companywide metrics meeting. It is less than thirty minutes, and we go through each of those metrics."

You need indicators to be confident that progress is being made toward the objective and to know when to step in to correct problems. A board of directors will want to see a valid and comprehensive set of indicators, so it can carry out its overall responsibility of assuring the organization's effective and efficient operations and achievement of results. In larger organizations, there are usually separate and independent monitoring and evaluation units. In all organizations, monitoring is a major responsibility of supervisors.

Monthly reports

Monthly reports are easier when an organization has key progress indicators that can be reflected in monthly counts. With good indicators, it is easy to indicate whether plans are on schedule and focus more on identifying problems and taking corrective action. Reports to the board are also easier to complete for the same reasons.

When I was executive director of a large nonprofit in the U.S., I asked for monthly reports from my top seven managers, no more than one page long with a simple comparison of progress versus plan in the top half of the page and then statements of any problems and recommendations in the bottom half. Managers preferred this reporting approach, because their reports were fast and easy to complete. These reports were functional and meaningful rather than bureaucratic. I also liked this approach, because it focused attention on important issues, saved preparation time for staff and review time for me, and avoided a lot of verbiage and explanation. I could also very easily convert these monthly reports into a summary report for my board of directors.

Actually drafting the operational plans – a day or longer as needed

Here is guidance to create operational plans for a department, unit, or individual with clear objectives and supporting text:

1. Each objective is a measurable result or accomplishment (as concise as possible).
2. It clearly contributes to the goals (self-evident or in just a few words).
3. The activities show progressive steps through the year (listing important activities).

4. Specific responsibilities, teams, or individuals are named for each activity.

5. Dates are indicated for each step to be completed (a specific date or by year end).

6. Key progress indicators are identified to assure you are on track and on time.

7. A reporting and evaluation system is included (by when, by whom, and to whom).

8. Resources, staffing, and support are indicated (as approved in the overall budget).

9. Baseline data and inputs into the planning are listed (as needed).

The operational plans for smaller organizations could consist of five to ten objectives in a one-page statement for each: the objective to be achieved with the activities, responsibilities, and deadlines.

During your planning, follow the steps below to create your organization's operational plans. I find it best when everyone is making their plans at the same time so there can be easy consultation and quick feedback with a clear deadline for all departments. The steps that follow are for Day Three of your strategic planning retreat. Of course, adapt these steps to your own situation. For larger organizations, a separate day soon after the retreat will be necessary to complete these steps.

Step 1: Review the agreed strategic directions

Good operational planning responds to identified problems and stakeholder expectations and takes steps to achieve agreed goals and objectives. To be successful, the operational plans build on the research findings and conclusions, with special attention given to stakeholders, what you want from them, and what they want from you. Keep the vision, mission, values, goals, and strategies visually available and top of mind as people draft their plans. This review is a good way to open the third day of the retreat to get everyone thinking in the same direction.

Step 2: Brainstorm possible objectives

I have seen it work well to have a plenary session for the entire planning group with everyone suggesting objectives for consideration. This is a free-flowing session with many suggestions for any function or department in the organization. It is creative and sometimes eye-opening to have program staff suggest objectives for fundraising, fundraising staff suggest objectives for program, and for all departments to interact with others. Alternatively, this work can be done in small groups, with each group providing feedback to the full group to create a comprehensive listing. The purpose here is to list a variety of *possible objectives* ranging from the reasonable to the very stretching for various functions of the organization.

The worksheet below can be used first to list possible objectives and, later, list the confirmed objectives for each department or team.

Step 3: Provide guidance on staffing, budgets, and other organization-wide considerations

The executive director and finance director present a framework for planning. This usually includes general staffing and budget guidelines and other information staff needs to have for appropriate planning.

P12 WORKSHEET: SUMMARY OF OPERATIONAL OBJECTIVES FOR _____ (department or unit) Check Possible __ or Confirmed__

What are our operational objectives for the coming year?

- Objectives state exactly what we want to achieve in the given planning period.
- Objectives flow directly from the strategic goals and applicable strategies.
- Objectives determine priorities and steps to contribute to strategic goals.
- An objective is a clear statement of a challenging, stretching, yet possible accomplishment.
- A good operational plan indicates how it contributes to the strategic goals.
- An objective and its activities should be drafted by those who will carry out the work.
- The director or supervisor leads, monitors, and supports the planning and implementation.

Operational plans indicate specific objectives, activities, and resources needed for success.

Based on the strategic plan, our department or unit will achieve the following objectives:

1.
2.
3.
+

Step 4: Break into departments, teams, and units to develop specific operational plans

For optimal group work, each group should have four to seven members including the director or team leader and a facilitator/reporter. The brainstormed possible objectives (using the P12 worksheet) may initially include objectives that seem unrealistic or whimsical. These objectives are shared with department directors and unit heads to develop their plans. Based on the previous work, each group determines the main objectives for its department or unit. It is important to prioritize possible objectives and select ones that are important, stretching, and achievable. Each group develops tactics for its primary functions and also ways to support fundraising, program, and efficiency in order to prioritize growth in revenues and improvements in programs and operations.

Each group drafts the activities, individual responsibilities, deadlines, and indicators as well as the reporting, staffing, financial resources, and other resources required. If one department needs input from another department, this is negotiated during the process.

Complete as much of this operational planning as possible during the retreat and, at minimum, confirm the overall objectives and strategies for each department. Most likely, final drafts of the functional areas' operational plans will need to be completed after the retreat as a way to involve other staff who are not participating in the retreat.

Throughout the process, executive leadership supports the planning. The consultant and executive director go from one group to another to provide guidance and encouragement. Finance provides ongoing input on budgets and resources.

Step 5: Present a summary of each department's operational plans and review their contribution to strategic goals

After reports by the leader in each group, other participants can suggest possible revisions to assure the objectives support and complement each other across departments and functions. Keep in mind that each department may often have objectives that relate to several different strategic goals and key strategies.

Step 6: Discuss how management will monitor, support, and adjust the work as the year progresses

This is a key subject for the full planning group for an understanding of how the year will unfold. The executive team and finance department will analyze the plans and produce the proposed budget either at this meeting or shortly after the retreat.

Step 7: Set the framework for a mid-year review to make appropriate updates and adjustments

Schedule a date for the mid-term review, so people will be prepared. Key progress indicators are needed to know how you are progressing and what changes may be needed after the mid-year review.

Step 8: Discuss follow-up plans for after the retreat

After the retreat, planning by staff should be completed within the next few days or week and involve everyone in the different departments or teams.

If you have not yet addressed organization culture, you should do this as soon after the retreat as possible. Note that you can do the operational planning even if you haven't determined your new, desired culture. Just assume the culture will be supportive. Later, you can determine exactly what you will need from your new culture.

The organization's overall or topline operational plan includes summaries of each department's objectives and budget – taken from the individual operational plan for each functional area. Finally, remember to celebrate a successful retreat!

At-a-glance steps to create operational plans during your strategic planning retreat

1. Review the overall strategic directions as the basis for operational planning.
2. Conduct a brainstorming session to generate possible objectives for the year.
3. Present overall staffing and budgetary guidelines for the planning.
4. Gather participants into department or functional groups to draft their operational plans.
5. Review in full session the plans from each department and their contribution to the goals.
6. Units and individuals develop plans to support their department goals and objectives.
7. Present how management will monitor, support, and adjust the work during the year.
8. Set the framework for a mid-term review to make appropriate updates and adjustments.
9. Discuss the next steps after the retreat.

Objectives for organization development and capacity building

Plans for organization development and capacity building activities should be included in the operational plans, along with the plans for program, funding, finance/administration, and other core functions. At the International Federation of Red Cross and Red Crescent Societies, we defined *capacity building* as improvements in the ability to deliver programs. We defined *organization development* as improvements in the organization's own functioning. This makes sense to me now, years after serving as head of organizational development at the Federation, because the purpose of a nonprofit organization is to deliver programs for the benefit of society, and its capacity to deliver programs is essential. Organization development, on the other hand, is focused on the organization itself and deals with governance, leadership, management, fundraising, finance, and other components of an organization that enable it to perform well.

Both organization development *and* capacity building *are important for every organization. If you did not address these two topics in previous steps (goals and key strategies), be sure to do so in your operational plans.*

Organizational development and capacity building are key to strengthening every organization. Some examples of organizational development are training staff to take on new responsibilities, creating a monitoring and evaluation unit, strengthening the board of directors, or initiating leadership development, management training, and other improvements needed to progress. Some examples of capacity building are improving the quality of program delivery, adding a supplemental service to assist beneficiaries, or establishing partnerships with appropriate community groups.

Completing your operational plans

Operational plans usually cover one fiscal year. If this is the first time you are creating operational plans, your plans can cover the remaining months to the end of the fiscal year.

The operational plans for a smaller nonprofit or community association do not need to be complex. For example, my neighborhood association engaged residents to develop simple, clear, and significant operational plans. It took about an hour to identify and plan an important activity such as graffiti removal, a neighborhood art show, or a cleanup project to be implemented by interested residents. A single evening meeting could produce five or more operational plans.

Obviously, operational plans are longer, more numerous, and more complex for larger nonprofits. When I heard a panel of experts from very large organizations talking about planning at an NGO forum, I was amazed and pleased to see that the presenters all held the title of vice president of strategy. Their plans were substantive and professional.

P13 WORKSHEET: OPERATIONAL PLANS FOR
_____ DEPARTMENT

Use this format for different objectives.

Objective: To _____

Activities: Person/Team responsible: Deadline:

1.

2.

3.

4.

5.

6.

7.

+

Key progress indicators (to know we are making progress):

1.

2.

3.

Support and resources needed:

Reasons this might not succeed – and what to do about it:

Overall supervision responsibility and reporting process:

Additional considerations:

Questions for implementation

1. Are you prepared to lead the process to generate exciting, stretching, achievable objectives for all departments, units, and individuals? What more do you need?

2. How will you know your participants have a clear know-how for operational planning including using worksheets P12 and P13? What will you do if they don't?

3. Can you provide the ongoing guidance needed to help groups and individuals improve plans that are not adequate? Who can help you in this process?

"We're almost finished with our individual plans for the year."

"When we know the overall goals and objectives, it's not that hard to do."

PART IV

Let's do it –
Creating strong values
and desired culture to
inform all you do

Plans are essential, but without strong core values and supporting culture, they will fail. That is why it is absolutely critical to assure you have identified strong core values and create a culture that will help you achieve the results you desire in your strategic and operational plans. This section provides the leadership and facilitation guidance to assure the strong values and involving culture you need for your nonprofit organization or community association.

For context, here is how all the pieces fit together:

1. *Vision* for a better world that inspires others to join you in your shared dreams

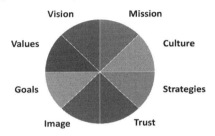

2. *Mission* that empowers everyone to move the vision to desired results

3. *Core values* that you believe most deeply as the fundamentals that guide you in everything

4. *Strategic goals* that you must achieve in three to five years to succeed in your work

5. *Key strategies* as "how" to reach your goals and objectives and to meet stakeholder needs

6. *Positioning* to clarify how others see your organization – different, special, and appealing

7. *Trustworthiness* or *credibility* as essential attributes – why people should trust you

8. *Organization culture* so you behave and work together for success

---

Build your culture on your strong core values. Let your values and culture strengthen your program, public relations, and advocacy.

10

Understanding organization culture as reality and making it strategy

Having the right organization culture is a key strategy to achieve your desired results. Strategy tells you how you will work together to achieve your goals and objectives. Organization culture is the "strategy" that tells you how you behave. It is integrally interwoven with all other key elements of your organization including your strategic plan, operational plans, and day-to-day activities.

In reality, even if the culture is not clearly articulated, it exists. It will be either unifying and supporting or divisive and counterproductive. Unless you make an effort to clarify the overall culture, the different subcultures that likely exist in different parts of your organization, such as fundraising versus program, will lead to group conflict. An unexamined culture is like an unkempt, messy, disorganized, self-conflicted person – difficult or impossible to work with.

Without an involving and supporting culture, your plans are missing a key component of how to work together to do it all. A unifying organization culture will help everyone work better together.

However, in any organization, you need a strategic plan before you develop the culture to support it. People need to know what you want to accomplish and the results you want before they can successfully address the culture needed to "oil" the process. In an article in *Fortune*, Steve Howe of Ernst & Young stressed this point exactly: "To improve its culture, a company must first define its purpose. Why does it exist, and what greater good does it serve?" Before you address culture, of course, you also need to have your updated core values statement.

The strategic plan says what you want to do. Your culture statement says how you will behave to get it done.
Will your culture be oil or sand in your plans?

When you develop a clear organization culture, it binds your organization together and unites everyone in their work together. This facilitates common pursuit and support of agreed goals in all fundraising, administration, and program work for the entire organization. Certainly, in any organization there will be debate, discussion, and even disagreement, but all this will be done in harmony and with commitment to achieve success by working together – as long as everyone is working under the umbrella of a clear organization culture statement.

The culture of an organization shines through as its personality

Similar to national culture, the culture of an organization is made up of the values, beliefs, assumptions, and norms of the members of the organization and reflects their behaviors, internally and externally. You can tell a culture by what people talk about, what they smile about, and what they criticize. It is demonstrated in the rewards at staff meetings, attitudes about donors and beneficiaries, stories about the organization, and most especially the comments at the end of a bad day. The culture is how the organization operates – specifically its cooperation and coordination, its efficiency in working together, and the relationships between staff, board, and volunteers – literally how the organization works together.

In their book *The Charismatic Organization*, Shirley Sagawa and Deborah Jospin describe culture as an organization's personality or character: an organic system of shared beliefs, values, assumptions, expectations, and norms that indirectly dictate attitudes and behavior and endure even as people leave and others take their place.

Because culture dictates the rules of behavior and can inhibit or encourage practices important to achieving an organization's mission, Sagawa and Jospin believe that a values statement should be reflected in the culture, telling people what is sacred. This integrates values into culture. They offer some examples of key concepts, useful for any nonprofit organization:

- Courage: "We are willing to take risks and stand up for principle."
- Creativity: "We always look for a new and better way and have fun while doing it."
- Equality: "Everyone is valued and respected regardless of background or position."
- Quality: "We aim to be the best at everything we do."
- Integrity: "We do what is right, not what is easy."
- Potential: "We believe every person can succeed with the right help."

Having a clear organization culture lets people know what is expected of them

Culture clearly delineates and guides how people are to behave, literally minute by minute and in every interaction, thereby reducing friction and conflict. When staff see the culture highlighted in posters and modeled by the leaders and champions, they learn to work and behave within the same cultural boundaries. In some for-profit companies, the culture is "winners take all" while in others the culture is based on teamwork. Nonprofit organizations are generally more driven by teamwork and their mission, but their culture determines how they do that.

The results of clarifying and improving your organization's culture can be significant. The benefits of taking time for "culture work" include gaining a shared understanding of the importance of having a common culture, reaping the benefits of more effective and more efficient work, and creating a more efficient organization overall, with more funds raised and superior program impact.

The outputs, outcomes, and impacts from a clear and supporting culture

In planning, it is important to distinguish outputs, outcomes, and impacts. Here are some tips I have found to be helpful when discussing the culture an organization needs to support the vision, mission, goals, and operational plans:

1. The expected *outputs* are a better understanding by everyone of the importance of a healthy, productive culture; clarifying how you want to work together now and into the future; and gaining commitment to translate agreed values and culture into working smoothly together to achieve objectives.

2. The expected *outcomes* are reduced conflict and wasted time; more productive work individually and as teams; increased satisfaction for staff, board members, and volunteers; and better fundraising, management, and program work.

3. The expected *impacts* (results) are a more efficient and more effective organization, more funds raised, more productive partnerships, more motivated staff, better program results, and greater success.

Culture is the glue that binds a group of people together

A well-tuned organization culture combines vision, mission, values, and people. Good culture requires commitment by everyone to live it and support it. It may take six months or longer with leadership and persistence to fully achieve your new, desired culture.

Good culture will:

- Unify everyone in their work
- Reduce stress and disagreement
- Give staff a similar way of behaving
- Facilitate pursuit of common objectives
- Prevent undermining plans and activities
- Make work cooperative and not conflicted
- Provide the lubricant to achieve goals and objectives

Example 1: How culture changed a small community organization – and an entire neighborhood

This is a story of how changing the culture changed an entire organization. My wife Rebecca and I were living in an economically diverse neighborhood in Providence, Rhode Island, USA. It had a diverse population and a large number of historic homes from the nineteenth century, which were the two main reasons we were living there. It also had serious problems with litter, graffiti, crime, drugs, and abandoned houses.

Late one night we were awakened by a crash through our downstairs window, our wildly barking dog, and screaming fire alarms. We ran downstairs, called the fire department, and tried to beat out the flames on the dining room table. Someone had thrown a firebomb, a Molotov cocktail, through our front window! Firefighters arrived within minutes, and the physical damage was relatively minimal. However, for the following weeks we could not sleep due to a powerful fear of repetition! We decided we had to leave to escape – or do something to improve the neighborhood.

We chose the neighborhood. There happened to be a meeting of the West Broadway Neighborhood Association (WBNA) shortly after the firebombing, and we attended. There were board elections that night and, on the spur of the moment, I decided to volunteer. I was elected to the board and then to chair the board, and Rebecca stepped up to be consultant and facilitator of teambuilding processes.

The initial leaders of the association appreciated the beauty of the neighborhood and its historic buildings and had attracted a number of new homeowners. They had created an important organization but had not been able to reach out more broadly into the community. For several years, planning activities in the association had been ad hoc, just responding to problems. The main "activities" at meetings were complaining about the conditions in the neighborhood and criticizing city authorities. The culture of this organization was, in a few words, negative, depressed, and helpless. Not surprisingly, membership and participation were small. The revenue, activities, and impact were not very big. It was an organization with a great dream of a better neighborhood but with no strategic plan, operational plans, or effective culture – and with limited results.

We set out to establish a new way for the organization to work, especially in what happens at its meetings and follow-up activities.

Everyone wanted to have better conditions in the community, they just didn't know how. We changed that dynamic. For example, when someone presented a complaint or criticism, instead of joining in the complaining, we would turn the complaint into a challenge – and then turn the challenge into an opportunity – and then turn the opportunity into a plan.

We would ask that person whether he or she wanted to do something about the problem and, if so, would immediately form a small group with others who agreed to sit together for half an hour to develop a response to the problem. With good facilitation, that is all it took for a group to draft a short but significant plan of action. Over the course of several meetings, we did this for the dozen major complaints about the neighborhood. These small plans soon became part of a bigger plan.

At the next meetings, we focused on developing sections of what became the larger strategic plan for the association. We took time to develop answers for these questions:

- What is our vision for the neighborhood?
- What is our work going to be?
- What values guide us?
- How are we going to do that work?
- How do we reach out to others to involve them?

Within a few months, we developed a simple but challenging strategic and operational plan for the next three years. We crafted powerful statements for our vision, mission, values, strategic goals, key strategies, and objectives. And we built small but committed work teams. The participation at meetings increased, because people heard we had stopped complaining and were doing meaningful things. Soon there were activities every week and every month – crime alerts, graffiti removal, street signs, art exhibits, cleanup events, a festival, and more. Based on our new strategic plan, we received a $100,000 grant from a major local foundation.

In this process, what we actually did was change the culture of the association and its meetings from complaining to problem solving and from helplessness to "We can do that!" The culture of the organization became positive and confident, because partic-

> ## A "CAN DO" Culture for a Community Association
>
> **Complaint → Challenge → Opportunity → Plan**
>
> **Excitement → Involvement → Activity → Impact**

ipants identified what they wanted to do and gained confidence in their ability to do it. Meetings became productive and fun!

We were changing the neighborhood by developing plans, implementing activities, and reaching out to involve others. We made the meetings positive and productive, and we were actually getting results! It all hinged on the new culture for this association to move from complaint to challenge, from challenge to opportunity, and from opportunity to a plan of action – and empowering the community.

There was one individual, for example, who hated graffiti. He saw graffiti for what it was – ugly markings by gangs to control turf and promote illegal activities. Every Saturday morning, he would go from house to house with a wagonload of paints and brushes. He would talk to homeowners and residents and tell them about the negative effects of graffiti on the beauty, values, safety, reputation, and self-image of the neighborhood. With their permission, and usually with their help, he would remove or paint over any graffiti on their property. Over the weeks, more and more people would join him, and eventually this team covered the entire neighborhood.

The "can do" culture of the meetings spread to his anti-graffiti work, and his success spread to other residents who started caring more for their own property. Within a year, graffiti disappeared from the neighborhood! When I visited several years later, it was (and still is today) a beautiful, historic district with people of diverse incomes and diverse backgrounds living in historic buildings with virtually no graffiti.

With a good plan, structured activities, and positive culture, the organization was able to achieve significant results. Word of our approach spread. The mayor called me and said he heard the meetings were good with lots of participation and positive energy. He asked if he could come to the next community meeting. I told him, "No!" Then I added, "That is, not unless you bring your police chief with you, because we have a neighborhood plan to work with the city for a safer neighborhood. Can you do this?" Over the next six months the mayor attended meetings quite often and always brought a senior official with him: the sanitation manager, the fire chief, the building inspector, and, yes, the police chief.

At a typical meeting, a group of residents would tell the mayor and his chief aide about a particular problem along with their assessment, plans, and recommendations for both the neighborhood and the authorities. For example, with the police chief, we explained that we were starting a neighborhood crime-watch program, and we wanted police officers to be on foot or on bikes in our neighborhood rather than driving around in patrol cars. The mayor and our group worked together with other officials to get state and federal funding for a "cops on bikes" program. After one year, my wife and I moved to Geneva, Switzerland, for new work opportunities and, just a year later when I visited, police officers were on foot and on bikes. They were clearly taking time to get to know the neighborhood and its residents. Because this small neighborhood association was organized, productive, and positive, the mayor responded and conditions changed.

On the income side, the approach was equally successful. Many more members joined and their dues increased the budget. We received sponsorship and funding from the mayor, the Rhode Island Foundation, a large corporation, and local organizations for a neighborhood festival, organizational development, a playground, and other activities and projects. In only twelve months the association's budget jumped from $3,000 to $200,000!

A few years after my wife and I moved, I received an update from an association member who reported that the budget now was above $1 million from private and public sources including membership, individual contributions, proceeds from events, corporate sponsorship, and government grants. Imagine growing your nonprofit or community association's annual budget from $3,000 to $1 million in just a few years!

West Broadway Neighborhood Association

Year	1992	1993
• Culture	Negative	Positive
• Planning	Ad hoc	3 year strategic plan
• Participation	Limited	Open / Extensive
• Activities	Complaining	Doing / Getting results
• Influence	Little	Significant
• Members	25	200+
• Revenues	$3,000	$200,000+

And now it is changing the city of Providence with millions of dollars!

https:www.wbna.org

The most gratifying part of this update, however, was confirmation that the association was using the same planning process, living the same "can do" culture, and achieving important impacts in the community. It was known as the best neighborhood association in the city, and board members started advising other neighborhood associations. I know that none of the plans, none of the outreach to the community, and none of the work with the authorities would have succeeded unless the organization culture had become positive and "can do," along with effective leadership. That made all the difference.

Our neighborhood and the entire city benefited from my strategic planning approach. The mayor of Providence, Rhode Island, issued a proclamation that "Kenneth H. Phillips has provided an invaluable service to the West Broadway Neighborhood Association and the City of Providence through his leadership and guidance … forging a clear path upon which the WBNA can continue to improve the quality of life in the West Broadway Neighborhood." How gratifying!

Successful culture change in a small organization (West Broadway Neighborhood Association)

Old culture:	New culture:
1. Complaining about issues	1. Building on possibilities
2. Negative	2. Positive
3. Helpless	3. A "can do" attitude

Example 2: How culture enabled a large international organization to triple its revenue

In 1982, I was hired to become the national executive director of Foster Parents Plan, also known as PLAN International USA. The organization had experienced ten years of no growth, with its annual revenue stuck at $10 million, its donor base stagnant, and its innovative spirit long gone. I was brought on with a specific mandate to increase the fundraising results of the organization as soon as possible.

The 110 staff members were committed and smart but undirected and disheartened. The board members were nice but not particularly skilled for the challenges we faced. The first step we undertook was a comprehensive situation assessment including market research, which led to a well-crafted, three-year strategic plan with a stretching growth strategy. The key elements of the strategic fundraising plan were to focus the first year on finding meaningful breakthroughs in fundraising and marketing, improve and roll out the successful tests in a large way in the second year, and dramatically increase the fundraising budget in the third year – all designed to double the income to $20 million in three years. The planning was good, and the board approved the plan.

However, I discovered a big barrier: The organization culture was rife with a sense of helplessness and an attitude of "We tried that, and it failed." Initially, I used a top-down leadership style with a culture that I defined as being innovative, learning, confident, and committed to change, with strong leadership on my part. This approach was successful as staff bought into this culture. The staff developed competence and confidence, and we did make significant progress.

Part way through this process and wanting more staff initiative, we organized a two-day staff retreat to address culture as a barrier. An excellent external consultant facilitated the process. In small groups and then in the full group with all 110 of us, together we identified the current culture:

- Committed to the mission
- Stuck in the past
- Critical attitudes
- Unable to make improvements

Next, we used a detailed process, as shown later, to identify the key components of the new, desired culture, a culture that would support the stretching new plans. In the meeting, we identified the new culture as:

- Passion for the mission
- Obsession with growth
- Commitment to donor service

Several staff members objected to the terms *passion* and *obsession*. I felt it was important to include them, and we debated this for some time. When it became clear that the majority of the staff were ready to accept this description of our new, desired culture, the consultant who was facilitating our process intervened and said to the several objectors, "The train is leaving the station, and you have a choice to be on the train or to get off, but you cannot stop the train from leaving any longer." The objectors fell silent, and the terms for the emerging new culture were broadly endorsed. *Lesson 1: Sometimes you need to tell resisters to get with the group and stop resisting.* This was the first of four powerful lessons I learned that day!

But we weren't done. A young employee who had not said anything in our meeting stood and, addressing me directly, said, "I don't know who you are. You spend all your time with managers and board members talking about plans and strategies. You never come to see what I do. I don't feel appreciated. I just wish …." She looked out the window and quietly continued, "I just wish I felt like a flower on a sunny spring day when I'm here at work." Wow! I was taken aback, far more by her quiet intervention than by the loud but recently silenced resisters.

The consultant then led me into a very personal exploration to make a candid statement to everyone about who I am, how I think, my passion for the organization, what I wanted to achieve, and how

I could change myself in this new culture. The result of this intervention was my realization that I had not opened myself up to others and had not provided enough appreciation to staff for what they were doing – and that my lack of openness and appreciation was reflected in the behavior of others. I had been reinforcing the negative, critical part of our culture!

I suggested we adopt as the fourth component of our desired culture the following phrase that I still really love: "Let everyone shine!" This was enthusiastically endorsed by everyone in the room. *Lesson 2: Get everyone involved and listen to them to determine your new, desired culture. And open yourself to the changes you need.*

Over the next weeks we put signs in hallways and offices highlighting the new culture. We put a bell in the middle of meeting tables for people to ring when someone – anyone – did not live up to the culture. Managers reminded their colleagues how to live the culture. Individual action plans included a section on reinforcing the culture. Performance appraisals included a self-assessment and then supervisory review of how each individual supported the culture. We truly focused on letting everyone open up and shine. And it worked. Everyone followed the

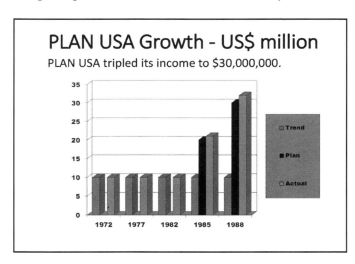

new culture, and I changed also, especially in how I spent my time in the office and how I supported the rest of the staff.

The increase in the fundraising results came largely through a "test — discover — expand" marketing strategy for growth with a lot of innovation and big leaps in strategic thinking. We explored a new name, Childreach, to work better in the marketplace. The culture was the oil that made the strategic plan and operational plans work so well. Our exciting, new culture encouraged everyone to find new ways to support fundraising results, reduce costs, and make other improvements. *Lesson 3: Put in place policies and practices to reinforce the new culture.*

At a board meeting at the end of the first three-year strategic plan, we presented results showing that we had slightly exceeded the objective of doubling our income to $20 million in those three years. The board actually applauded at the end of my presentation. And we moved on to the next strategic plan with the same approach, with astonishing results. In six years, we were able to:

- Increase the number of donors from 30,000 to 100,000
- Increase revenues from $10 million to $30 million (about $64 million in current value)
- Increase internal efficiency to get more done with lower costs for administration

A huge increase in staff efficiency came about because of the continuous-improvement approach by the finance/administration director in which staff analyzed and improved their use of time, their work, and paper flow. New technology helped as well. We inspired and rewarded staff members for their suggestions. We encouraged everyone to shine. The planning, culture, and commitment led to significant improvements in productivity, so 25 percent fewer staff in the fundraising, finance/administration, and donor relations departments were able to manage their work very well even with the increase in revenues, the tripling of donors, and expanded activities in education and advocacy.

The new, high-energy culture gave staff more confidence, more independence and, I think, more satisfaction in their work. At my recent birthday gathering, I met with half a dozen former colleagues and heard their excitement and praise for what we were all able to accomplish at this organization. For example, from Donna Jean Rainville, former director of finance and administration: "Ken, thanks for leading a legendary team that brought PLAN USA to new heights. It was a pleasure to have been on the ride!" *Lesson 4: Let everyone on staff flourish. It was the amazing staff who always stepped up to lead in so many ways that led to our success.*

People matter! Culture matters!

Successful culture change in a large organization (Foster Parents Plan/PLAN International USA)

Old culture:	New culture:
1. Committed to the mission	1. Passion for the mission
2. Stuck in the past	2. Obsession with growth
3. Critical attitudes	3. Commitment to donor service
4. Unable to make improvements	4. Let everyone shine!

Questions for implementation

1. Examples of the expected outputs when working to improve organization culture include a better understanding by everyone of the importance of a healthy, cooperative culture; clarifying how you want to work together; and gaining commitment to translate agreed values and culture into working together to achieve objectives. In a few words, what are the specific outputs you hope to achieve?

2. Examples of the expected outcomes include reduced conflict and wasted time; more productive work individually and as teams; increased satisfaction for staff, board members, and volunteers; and better fundraising, management, and program work. In a few words, what are the specific outcomes you hope to achieve?

3. Examples of the expected impacts include a more efficient and more effective organization, energized staff, more funds raised, more productive partnerships, more advocacy, better program results, and greater success. In a few words, what are the specific impacts you hope to achieve?

Now you can see if you have any sand left in your culture.

11

Assessing and then designing the values and culture you need – Essential Work

The right, strong values coupled with an involving, supporting culture will inspire and empower your staff, leaders, board members, volunteers, and others to support your organization's strategic plans with energy and commitment. On the other hand, a culture that is stuck, negative, or blaming will undermine (or even sabotage) those plans. And values that are weak will not serve to strengthen your culture.

For nonprofits, the challenge in having a healthy culture may come from differing management styles of leaders, conflicts between different departments (especially fundraising and program), not addressing the culture issue effectively, or contradictory attitudes between board members and staff. This discord results in strong opinions held by different individuals or even units, because there is no unifying statement or commitment for the culture.

If an organization fails to promote strong, clear values and the desired culture to support its plans, clashes among individuals, functions, or subgroups are inevitable as well as clashes between different executives or between board members and

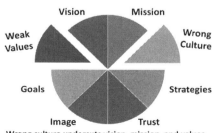

Wrong culture undercuts vision, mission, and values.
Weak values sabotages goals, strategies, and image.

staff. The solution is good planning with full participation to achieve a unified culture.

In this chapter, you and your staff will assess current culture and design your new, desired culture. In addition to the guidance presented here, I encourage you to download and use the tools I developed and refined over many years while consulting with hundreds of nonprofits in dozens of countries: "Assessing Your Core Values and Organization Culture." You can download this tool from my website (www.NGOFutures.com) to work with your entire staff to create the culture you want and need. Since strong core values are the basis of organization culture, you first need to look more closely at your values and then address culture.

This planning tool includes sections to address issues of values and culture. Using this tool and following the instructions in this chapter, participants will:

1. Revisit and update your core values to assure they are strong enough to confront the challenges you encounter internally and externally.

2. Examine national culture as an example and introduction to assessing your own organization culture.

3. Individually, begin to identify the components of how the organization as a whole behaves now.

4. Then in small groups and finally together, reach conclusions about your current culture, both the good and bad.

5. Individually, then in small groups, then collectively – and based on your vision, mission, and values – identify the components of the new, desired culture you need to achieve agreed goals and objectives.

6. Identify possible barriers that might prevent you from achieving the desired changes and successful implementation of the identified new culture.

7. Recommend solutions to overcome those barriers and draft a plan of action to implement the new culture to assure progress and success.

8. Identify and plan how to use your strong values and involving culture to support your programs, advocacy, and public communications.

When I facilitate strategic planning retreats for most nonprofit organizations, I prefer to include the culture discussion near the end of Day Two. (You'll see this reflected in the template agenda for a three-day strategic planning retreat in Appendix 3.)

However, larger organizations require more time to address organization culture – perhaps a three-hour morning or afternoon session. If you have a large organization with many staff, your culture session could take most of the day, since it would involve more small groups with more feedback and consensus-building sessions. It is important to involve all staff, if possible. Globally dispersed organizations should include enough representatives so all staff will feel involved. A community organization can usually do this in a single evening session.

In all cases, I have found that doing much of the work in small groups of five to seven participants gets more involvement from each person, actually speeds up the discussion process, and produces the best conclusions. In the full-group session, feedback from the different groups is often eye-opening for everyone. You will see many common views and hear other views, which merit further discussion.

In my experience, diverse groups tend to yield the best discussion results, so I prefer to have groups with different functions represented. Alternatively, I opt for the random approach to create groups, because it is a quick way to create small groups with diverse members. When diverse groups wrestle with different perspectives – reflecting their different functions as they work to create consensus for feedback to the full group – this can spur interesting discussions with effective results.

Start by confirming the core values and assuring they are strong enough

After convening the staff (as well as some board members and key volunteers, if you can), you should give a preview of what you will be doing along with definitions of values and culture and why getting these foundational concepts right is so important to achieve the results you have identified in your strategic plan. I recommend distributing the values and culture planning document from my website as the working tool for this session, and using it in conjunction with the steps presented below. Also, you may want to read again the discussion of core values and recommended steps to arrive at a values statement, presented in Chapter 4.

Although you may have already addressed values early in the planning along with vision and mission, it is still definitely useful to review values more thoroughly along with culture at this point in the planning process. It is important to give staff and other stakeholders the opportunity to review and consider them in group discussions.

Note that some portions of your values statement may not change. For example, a faith-based organization is not going to change its faith just because it has a new strategic plan. A child-focused nonprofit will not change its values about the importance of children. A pro-democracy organization is not going to change its values just because there is a new government in place.

Just as political hot topics inspire passion and activism, your strong core values will inspire people to be passionate, committed, and active in your cause. Thanks to your strong values, they will flock to your organization.

Core values are what you believe most deeply as the fundamentals that guide you in everything. *Strong* core values are more likely to carry over meaningfully and strengthen programs, advocacy, and public communications.

An example of adhering to strong core values was presented in an August 2020 news report about a police department in Georgia that fired one of its police officers. The officer tasered a woman who was resisting arrest for a relatively minor incident. After reviewing the incident (including a video taken by a neighbor), the department fired the officer, because he "did not meet our core values." The official report by the Gwinnett County Police Department includes the following statement: "One of our core values is courtesy. We strive to conduct ourselves in a manner that promotes mutual respect with the community and our peers. The investigation in this case has shown that this officer violated our policy and did not meet our core values." This is a great example of strong core values in the workplace. Remarkable!

To break new ground, revisit and update your values statement to ensure they are strong core values, particularly if you are going through significant organizational change such as adopting an innovative strategic plan, changing your program focus, moving from program to advocacy, dramatically increasing your fundraising effort, or responding to major shifts in society.

In the cases of significant change, the leadership often has to stand firm, insisting on new or clarified values that support the overall plan. Examples could be: "Yes, we are closing our programs and focusing on advocacy – and strength of conviction is a new core value" or "Yes, we are changing our work from community control to community support – and courtesy is a new core value." In these situations, leadership must guide staff to understand and embrace the new core values, especially when you are responding to significant social or organizational changes.

Even with difficult topics, small-group discussion allows for more participation, involvement, and acceptance or commitment. Throughout the process, the views of the leader or founder are especially significant, but, in all cases, this person must be careful not to short-circuit the process. It is important to encourage candor and honesty, as open discussion may reveal discrepancies in what the leaders believe the values are and what others experience them to be, or the staff may not understand the higher values at play and the absolute need for change.

If such discrepancy exists, it is far better to address it rather than leave it undiscussed and unresolved as a festering problem and, worse, as an example of hypocrisy on the part of the organization's leaders or something that will prompt sabotage on the part of unaccepting staff. I always find it facilitates progress to view this discussion not as prompting conflicts but rather as an essential way to move forward for the good of the organization and of society.

As noted earlier, it is wise to select five or six strong core values. If you have more than eight, they cease to be memorable. What is not memorable is easily lost. Too many values will become just another list and will have less impact in reality. If you need to reduce the number, combine some values that are similar. Use your own stories and experiences and those presented in this book along with a broader sense of social significance to identify the most important values that actually should guide behavior. Your final values statement should reflect what the organization leaders and staff and your key stakeholders really believe are your most fundamental values now and into the future.

If your values are *strong* core values, they will strengthen your programs, advocacy, and public communications. They will fuse your staff into a cohesive, powerful team even in the face of controversy, criticism, and counterattacks. And they will energize stakeholders – board members, staff, volunteers, donors, and others – in efforts to achieve your goals and mission.

It will be useful to put the draft core values statement in a Power-Point slide for projection or a poster for easy reference and guidance as you proceed. At the end of the planning, your values statement should be included or reflected in all your strategic and operational plans, staff meetings, public communications, funding proposals, advocacy, and program activities.

Consider national culture as a model

Now we turn our attention from values to culture. Before talking about organization culture, I find it is helpful to focus on national cultures as a model of what culture really is. In this simple and fairly short exercise, participants identify the key traits in their own national culture and compare them to those of another culture. (If you have any questions, it will help to review the discussion on organization culture in Chapters 5 and 10.) I would give this initial step about national culture twenty to thirty minutes at most. There is no need to reach conclusions or develop consensus. It is simply an introduction to the concept of organization culture.

What is your view of your organization's current culture?

To design a better culture, you need to truly understand the current culture. How do you fix a flat tire if you don't know which tire is flat? It's the same for culture. Using the planning tool ("Assessing Your Core Values and Organization Culture"), this activity guides participants to identify your organization's current culture first for each individual, then in small groups, and then in the full group. The task is to describe accurately your current culture as a bridge to drafting the desired culture. This should involve all staff or as many as possible.

I always remind the organization's leaders to call for full candor and honesty in this process and to demonstrate their respect for honesty by everyone, even if the comments sting. If there is a problem in the current culture and you don't identify it, the problem will remain – and possibly fester. Only by identifying a problem behavior will you be able to determine what needs to be done to make it better. Here is an example: "We have a culture of blame (and it starts at the top)." Working in small groups also helps by providing time to talk and offers some anonymity in the process. You do want to know the good and bad about your culture.

Organization culture is how you behave and how you work together. An energizing, involving, supporting culture is necessary for success.

To identify the elements in your current culture, both good and bad, I find the best and quickest way is for each person, individually, to look at a list of behaviors and identify those that are most predominant on a day-to-day basis in their work. Specifically, identify behaviors that facilitate your work and behaviors that inhibit progress in your work.

The "Assessing Your Core Values and Organization Culture" tool provides a list of fifty-four traits or behaviors. Participants can check off a reasonably small number of traits in the NOW column. They should include both good and bad behaviors that they experience as predominant in their day-to-day activity in the organization. Encourage participants to add other descriptors for your specific situation that are not on the list.

Ask each person to narrow down their list to the five to eight most significant or dominant behaviors they experience in the organization (both good and bad). Ask participants to keep these questions in mind as they select the behaviors they see as predominant:

- What do you say to yourself about how people are behaving?
- Which behaviors do you praise? Want to emulate?
- Which behaviors do you dislike? Complain about?
- Which behaviors are rewarded? Punished?
- How do the leaders treat others in meetings and in hallways?
- How do people sit, stand, and walk and what does that imply?
- What are the topics of gossip? What do people really like? Dislike?
- Which behaviors help you in your work? Hinder your work?
- Which behaviors do you brag about? Complain about?

After individuals identify key cultural traits from their own perspective, move on to the next step: small-group discussion.

What is the consensus about your current culture?

At this point, the small groups should discuss the behavior traits and develop a group consensus of the five to eight most common behaviors, both good and bad, as currently displayed in the organization.

Briefly, here are suggestions for an effective group process:

- A facilitator leads the process and a notetaker captures information, so everyone sees it.
- Participants take turns, keep their comments short, and listen to each other.
- The group develops a list of current behaviors including positive ones and negative ones.
- The group identifies the five to eight most dominant behaviors to report back to others.

When you reach consensus in the group, list the dominant behaviors you have identified including both those that facilitate progress and those that inhibit progress in daily work.

Now the small groups join together to create one large group. You might need a facilitator who would point to one group, then another, in turn, collecting one item at a time and keeping a master list for everyone to see. Work together to identify the consensus of the five to eight dominate behaviors currently displayed in the organization.

At this time in the process of moving forward, be sure to keep this discussion positive and even lighthearted as well as honest. Be careful not to dwell on specific negative experiences. The key is identifying the good aspects of your current culture that you will carry forward as well as those that need to change. Discussion may produce consensus or, eventually, a voting system may be needed to produce a final statement about the organization's current culture: How we behave now.

In the final statement, it is necessary to include both the good behaviors and those that are not good. To identify and design the new culture that really does provide oil for your daily workflow, you must identify any elements that tend to throw sand into your processes, so you can correct or modify those elements.

Changing a culture – especially getting rid of negative components from the past – takes clarity, honesty, and persistence. Adam Grant, professor at the Wharton School of the University of Pennsylvania, specializes in organizational psychology. He describes the importance of addressing the worst cultural traits:

- How just or unjust is the workplace?
- How secure or insecure are people in their work?
- How much control or lack of control do people have as they work?

These specific issues may or may not be relevant to your organization, but removing negative traits is certainly as important as preserving positive traits.

To create the culture you need, identify how you want to behave in the future

It is now time to identify your new, desired culture – the culture that will support your staff, board members, and volunteers to achieve your goals and objectives. In addressing and defining your desired culture, you should think of the external conditions, review your SWOT analysis, and focus on vision, mission, and values as well as your new strategic goals, key strategies, and objectives as you prepare to implement your strategic plan over the coming years.

This activity follows the same steps as the core values discussion – individual assessment, discussion and consensus in small groups, and feedback to the full group to get more complete consensus. But here the focus is on what kind of culture, what kind of behaviors that you, as individuals and as an organization, want to have in order to be a great place to work. How do you reflect your core values in your new, desired culture? How do you *really* need to behave individually, in teams, and with other departments to achieve the long-term results you have identified and agreed? What will you do to be productive, happy, smoothly functioning, and relatively stress-free? Specifically:

- Which good behaviors need to be preserved or strengthened?
- Which bad behaviors need to be eliminated?
- Which new behaviors are needed?

Surely with stretching objectives, you must have a culture that provides oil to your daily work and processes. You will certainly want to continue and possibly strengthen some of the behaviors identified in the current culture (the best ones that are still relevant and supporting) and to change others (the troublesome ones or those that are no longer important) to better or more appropriate behaviors. You should add any new behaviors that are needed. Certainly, you need to ground your culture in your strong core values.

Throughout this process, the organization's leaders need to demonstrate to the rest of the staff that they welcome candid appraisal, feedback, and recommendations. It is appropriate to consider the perspectives of both the leaders and the rest of the staff in the organization. The staff should hear and give special consideration to the views and concerns of leadership. And vice versa, the leaders need to hear and consider the views and concerns of everyone else. Only in this way will the organization get the culture it needs to achieve its goals, quite simply, because culture is for everyone.

The final statement of the new, desired organization culture emerges from individual reflection, small group work, leadership, and plenary consensus. Discussion should produce the consensus. As a last resort, a voting system may be needed to identify a short list of desired behaviors: *How we need to behave.*

Certainly, in any organization there will be debate and discussion and even disagreement but – when working in a clearly defined, supportive culture – all this will be done in harmony and with commitment to achieve greater success by working together. After people experience a culture process like this, I have seen strong pressure in a group to cooperate.

Based on open discussion and agreement by everyone involved, you now have a critical conclusion about how you want to behave in the future: *Your new organization culture.* This is huge!

This becomes your culture statement, and it is included in your strategic plan, operational plans, public communications, proposals, evaluations, website, meetings, posters for staff, and other important documents.

Identify possible barriers to living the new, desired culture

If you fail to identify possible barriers or fail to identify solutions to those barriers, your new culture will falter, and the old culture will undercut achievement in the new plans. The next two activities are to imagine what barriers might exist for the new culture to take root and then determine steps to overcome those barriers to establish the new culture firmly in the organization. These two activities – identifying the barriers and their solutions – are essential.

It is worth repeating here that changing culture is the most difficult process in the strategic planning process. Failure to create your new, desired culture most likely will lead to frustration, missed objectives, contentious meetings, and an unhappy workplace.

In fact, many large corporate mergers have failed simply because the cultures of the two merged corporations were so different and could not mesh together. In *6 Big Mergers That Were Killed by Culture*

(And How to Stop it from Killing Yours), Darcy Jacobsen offers a few pointers that are relevant to nonprofits looking to create their new, desired culture:

- Emphasize your core values – this will help you achieve growth and success.
- Any kind of change can produce negativity. Transform this into positivity by encouraging employees to "catch each other doing something right."
- Stop the brain drain by finding ways to ensure key leaders don't leave the organization, since this destabilizes the staff and drains confidence.
- Get buy-in from your most influential workers, since this can cause a wonderful ripple effect throughout the organization.
- Encourage communication between functional areas to strengthen these bonds.

In my consulting experience, after groups have successfully identified the new culture they want, I find they are generally excited and creative, since they understand that this new culture will make their work more productive, more rewarding, and more enjoyable. If your entire team is participating in the retreat – and if you have time in the agenda – it should be easy to get everyone involved to identify possible barriers that might prevent the successful implementation of your new, desired culture. As a reminder, this step is best undertaken when the organization's entire team is present and able to participate in this important discussion, since it is so important for everyone on the team to gain ownership in the new culture.

Right after the group has identified the new, desired culture, I ask everyone to suggest possible barriers. So, ask participants to think for a few minutes and write down possible barriers, then let everyone just call out their ideas in an open brainstorming process. In my work-shops, people mention things like "The board will not approve this," "I don't have time to do this," "You never really listen to me," and "The fundraising group keeps interfering in my program work." Capture the comments on a flip chart, combine similar ones, and aim to have a list of five to eight significant barriers. You can make this a fun activity. People really enjoy this open brainstorming process and the ability to be critical or funny or serious.

Identify solutions to overcome barriers

Next, determine the steps to overcome the barriers and establish the new culture firmly in the organization. Ask everyone to think for a few minutes about possible solutions and then start calling out some steps to take. Solutions might include: "We need the executive director's commitment to get everyone to live our culture." "We need to keep reminding ourselves that our new culture means we will spend less time disagreeing and more time being productive." "Having our new culture means we understand each other's work better – and can help each other more."

Make the identification of possible solutions fun. In my workshops, people often remember this session as a highlight! There can be a lot of laughter here. The result is a list of solutions and actions to overcome barriers.

At the end of your planning session, it is a good idea to create a "culture taskforce" to work together to develop the ideas to overcome potential barriers. The larger group has just identified the culture they want in the future and conducted an analysis of barriers and proposed solutions for success, and participants will feel good about that! They will be glad to approve a taskforce for the next steps. This can be a time to celebrate the good work on planning and culture!

Create a plan of action so the new culture will be embraced and lived

Making changes in culture is extremely difficult for most organizations. People may resist the change, or they may forget about their commitment to creating a new culture, because changing behavior is hard. Success requires strong leadership, creative support by champions, and dedication by others who are committed. In fact, success requires a plan of action to instill and reinforce the new culture.

If you have sufficiently involved staff in the culture work and based it truly on all the research and planning thus far, they should be supportive of living the new culture, simply because it will make their work easier and more successful.

The culture taskforce should draft and oversee a plan of action to remind everyone of the new, desired culture with ideas and actions to reinforce the agreed new behaviors. They should identify activities and procedures to reinforce and implement the culture based on suggestions and possible solutions to potential barriers. Activities could include posters of the culture statement in meeting rooms, reports in meetings, an activity related to culture in all individual plans, recognition of outstanding performances, and much more.

The taskforce can involve people at different levels to serve as early adopters and cheerleaders of the culture. These people support the culture change process, reinforce the new culture by their words and deeds, support it from different levels and departments of the organization, and encourage people to challenge others who fail to follow the new culture. These leaders are seen as champions or models of the new culture and generally have high credibility.

Culture champions help to overcome resistance by reminding everyone how the new culture improves workflow and gets better results in all areas of work. They can lead casual conversations and also stimulate serious discussions to promote progress:

- What are your impressions of progress so far on the culture?
- How are we interacting one-on-one to help create the new culture?
- How is culture impacting your work and how can we make it better?
- How can we make work more stress-free, more fun, and more productive?
- Are we getting rid of our bad behaviors and replacing them with better behaviors?

It is imperative that the organization's leaders demonstrate the new culture by being models of it.

Executives, directors, and managers must actively reinforce their support of the culture for the rest of the staff and include this in communications, feedback to staff, hiring decisions, orientation sessions, and awards and recognition.

As in any change process, it will take leading with the vision, communicating frequently and supportively, and managing for the results you want. This is true wherever you are in the organization's structure. I know it works – I've done this many times while working in many different positions.

The challenge of fundraising

When implementing a new culture change, I find that fundraising is often the area of greatest change.

An organization seeking to increase its financial resources to any significant degree and hoping to achieve real stability and sustainability (as all nonprofits should be doing) will need to plan for many substantial changes: new positioning and accountability in the marketplace, diversification of funding sources, increasing the overall effort and budget for fundraising, and new expertise in marketing and fundraising. Instilling a culture of fundraising usually requires involving executive leadership as well as the board of directors, new responsibilities for everyone in every department, developing an honorary board, and potentially tapping other external advocates to support fundraising and marketing. These are big changes.

A change process like this is often confusing and threatening to people who are used to doing work in the old way. Some staff may object, saying, "This is not my responsibility." This is why a plan of action to reinforce the new culture will help ensure the new, desired culture will take root. When we put a bell in the middle of the table for anyone to ring when someone (anyone) failed to follow the new culture, invariably this caused great laughter, embarrassment, and immediate correction to the desired behavior!

Occasionally, participants in a culture process ask me why we spend so much time to get consensus, especially what I call the "consensus of all of us." I do it to build agreement and solidarity. Consensus means everyone participated in the planning process and agreed to the big issues, so they are more likely to agree with the components of the new, desired culture – to achieve what they had already agreed. This is one reason I like to have everyone involved in the planning all the way through whenever possible – everyone has ownership in the process and the conclusions. Culture champions can remind others that "everyone participated and everyone agreed with the big issues. It's time to do it. The train is leaving the station."

Questions for implementation

1. The exercise to create your new, desired culture requires absolute honesty from all participants. How will you and your organizing team lead this process? Have you identified an internal or external facilitator who can effectively and objectively guide this discussion?

2. How can you encourage positive, open channels of communication and mutual support between functional areas, especially fundraising and program?

3. Several ideas were put forth in this chapter to overcome barriers to implementing your new, desired culture. How can you keep everyone's focus on your core values and new strategic goals to live up to your new culture?

"This has been an inspiring process! I now know
we can achieve great things … together."

12

Some models of core values and organization culture

Clearly, no two organizations are identical as they have widely varying visions, missions, and goals. They look to different donors and other stakeholders to help them make a better world. Therefore, it makes sense that organizations' values and culture statements will vary significantly. As a result, there is no single "right" way to present your values statement or publicly present your new culture.

With this in mind, I invite you to review the following examples of several organizations' fundamental documents. While I have mentioned several of the following organizations and highlighted a particular vision statement or list of core values, it is helpful to review each of these organization's guiding documents. Notice the differences and similarities. For example, one thing these documents have in common is brevity. As I noted earlier in this book, an organization's critical, driving document does not have to be lengthy or ponderous. Keep it short, inspiring, positive, and motivating!

Example 1: Global Alliance of Save the Children

- Positioning – Save the Children is the world's leading independent organization for children.
- Vision – A world in which every child attains the right to survival, protection, development, and participation.

- Mission – To inspire breakthroughs in the way the world treats children and to achieve immediate and lasting change in their lives.
- Values – Accountability, ambition, collaboration, creativity, integrity
- Programs – Humanitarian emergencies, health and nutrition, education, child protection, child rights, child poverty, and advocacy

Example 2: AIESEC Alumni International (AAI) as an example of coherence in plan-values-culture

The AIESEC alumni number one million people in business, education, nonprofits, and government around the world. When we come together, we meet in a common understanding and appreciation of each other. When I led a taskforce that drafted the alumni association's strategic plan, we realized we all have the same worldview, because we share the same values. What unifies an extremely large group representing so many different nationalities, professions, and ages? It is the organization's clear vision, values, and culture. I can travel anywhere in the world and find new colleagues and friends who are AIESEC alumni whom I respect and enjoy, because we share the same values and culture.

- The alumni vision is to unleash AIESEC's global alumni potential through structured, global, and cross-generational collaboration, so that AIESEC values are delivered for life.
- Our mission is to unite alumni around the world into an active global network and community, enhance our alumni's own professional and social lives, support and guide AIESEC, and advance leadership and international understanding for a better world.

- Our identity: We are a global network of AIESEC alumni with a lifelong commitment to further AIESEC's mission and to advance international leadership and understanding for a more unified world.
- Our core values as alumni are the shared AIESEC values: activating leadership, demonstrating integrity, living diversity, enjoying participation, striving for excellence, and acting sustainably.
- Our organization culture is: cooperative, supportive, and cohesive; ethical and professional; and sharing knowledge and experience.
- Our slogan: "Leadership under AIESEC values delivered for life."

Example 3: A large international organization in Geneva, Switzerland

I facilitated a process to improve the working culture in one department of a very large international organization in Geneva. The agenda for our meeting on culture was to discuss these topics: What is our culture now? What do we want it to be? What are the practical steps to implement our new, desired culture?

After small group discussions and plenary debates, the sixty participants agreed the current culture was: committed, based on principles, and hardworking but also donor-run, inward looking, blaming, firefighting, and dysfunctional. Clearly there were some great traits here as well as an urgent need for improvement.

Further work identified the new, desired culture as: mission-driven (committed, passionate, and based on principles); effective (focused, relevant, and learning); dynamic and responsive (innovative, creative, risk-taking but allowing and accepting failure); integrated (uniting, cooperating, and communicating); and positive (caring, nurturing, and supporting); inclusive (open, participatory, and culturally sensitive).

The goal of this planning session was to transform this organization into a more productive, effective, efficient, and pleasant place to work. Clearly, identifying this list of desired behaviors would support the creation of the organization's new, desired culture.

Example 4: A large nonprofit in Central Europe

This successful organization was planning to transition to a more diversified fundraising strategy. The transition to the new culture was simply an upgrade to higher performance.

Our values:
- Peace, kindness, integrity, honesty, hope in action
- Responsibility, knowledge, and skills
- Efficiency, diligence

Current organization culture:
- Dedicated and mission-driven
- Hardworking and competent with high expectations
- Responsible and accountable
- Sharing and willing to learn

New, desired organization culture:
- More creative and innovative
- More efficient
- More proactive, taking more initiative
- More able to assess and manage risks

Example 5: A global health organization

The global health organization that I supported developed its fundraising plan and culture as part of a new strategic approach and, as a result, increased revenues from $5 million to $20 million in a few years and to $60 million within a decade!

Current organization culture:
- Businesslike, entrepreneurial
- Scientific expertise (research and development), competence, dedicated
- Light, responsive, fast-acting, efficient, transparent, trustworthy
- Under-promise but over-deliver in the program
- Teamwork/Family
- Real concern for malaria/Mission commitment

Desired organization culture:
- Continuation of the current culture plus passion
- Valuing fundraising (the final frontier)/Valuing competence in fundraising
- Confident we will get the results/Knowing we have all the ingredients including fundraising
- Celebrating fundraising success/Money is good

Example 6: A mid-size American NGO

An organization looking to energize itself. Note the changes in the culture.

Old organization culture:
- Mission-driven
- Hardworking/committed

- Complacent/risk aversive
- Crisis mentality
- Deliberative/analytical
- Flat
- Flexible workplace

New, desired organization culture:
- Mission-driven and donor oriented
- Results oriented
- Entrepreneurial
- Disciplined
- Scientific
- Organized
- Flexible workplace

Example 7: Morristown-Beard School (my high school)

For this educational institution, the values statement starts with core values and concludes with culture (called moral principles).

"We continue to honor our longstanding core values (respect, responsibility, integrity, courage, compassion), and hereby incorporate them into a more expansive, updated statement of our ethical and social vision. The bedrock of our academic program is to provide a foundation in the liberal arts. Our most fundamental goal is to help train and guide our students, so they may ultimately contribute to making the world a better place, and we believe that all members of the MBS community should cultivate a life guided by moral principles, among them: awareness

of diverse perspectives, connectedness, cooperation, empathy, humility, humor, and independence of mind." The slogan (in Latin) translates to: "To the stars through difficulties/aspiration."

Example 8: A strategic plan for a community services organization for drug rehabilitation

This nonprofit service organization was concerned about relying on its large government contracts and wanted to develop its appeal for more diversified fundraising.

1. Our vision is a world where everyone in recovery is fully integrated into their communities and society sees the quality of life improve.

2. Our mission is to integrate people in recovery into their communities and improve the quality of their lives through mental health and substance abuse treatment.

3. Our new, desired organization culture:
   a. Focused on client care
   b. Committed to results
   c. Constant dialogue across all programs
   d. Dedicated to excellence through entrepreneurial spirit and hard work
   e. Accountability throughout the organization

4. We focus on residential and non-residential therapy, support, and skill development. We provide nurturing, therapeutic environments that offer a unique, intensive holistic treatment experience to serve the individual needs of mental health, substance abuse, and criminal justice clients.

5. Our critical issues:
    a. We lack needed skills, best practices, and staffing for programs, management, and fundraising.
    b. We don't have the money, buildings, or public relations we need.
    c. We don't have good measurements of our results.
    d. We are not accredited.
    e. We don't know if the strategic plan will work.

6. Our strategic goals:
    a. Develop new services and programs for new populations in greatest need.
    b. Develop skills, best practices, and staff for programs, management, and fundraising.
    c. Generate the funding we need.
    d. Develop good measurements of our results.
    e. Get accredited nationally.
    f. Build internal capacity to assure the strategic plan will work.

7. Our key organization strategies:
    a. Develop new programming to serve current and new clients
    b. Develop new sites for new programs
    c. Increase funding through more diversified and aggressive fundraising
    d. Increase public awareness and involvement
    e. Develop staff capacities to achieve organization goals
    f. Develop board capacities to achieve organization goals

8. Our fundraising strategy is to create a development (fundraising) program:
   a. Increase federal and state contract funding for programs through three new major funders
   b. Develop close collaborative relationship with major funders
   c. Develop municipal contacts for funding opportunities
   d. Generate 25 percent of our total income from the private sector from foundation and corporate grants and organization support
   e. Secure contributions from individuals and groups by holding various events, an annual appeal, planned giving, client fees for aftercare services, and one major annual fundraiser

9. The board of directors will address:
   a. A facilitated board self-assessment process
   b. Roles, responsibilities, terms, and procedures
   c. Strengthen board fundraising
   d. A fundraising committee
   e. New board members in fundraising
   f. Fundraising on each board agenda
   g. Ambassador and/or honorary board

Questions for implementation

1. If you reread the introduction to Part IV on values, do you see how your values can become key selling points in your services, advocacy, fundraising, and public relations?

2. Can you find models of strong values and supporting organization culture in other nonprofits that could inspire your team in creating stronger values and great culture for your organization?

3. In the examples presented in this chapter and others you find about values and culture, are there particular points that stand out as especially relevant, even inspiring, for your organization? How will you communicate them to the planning group?

PART V

After the planning – Implementing your plans, values, and culture

Creating your organization's strategic and operational plans – and strengthening values and identifying your new, desired culture – is no small feat. When you accomplish these monumental tasks, congratulations are in order!

Just as critical, however, is a new task: Implementation. Plans that are created and then filed away in a drawer, never to be seen again, are useless. Identifying your new culture without a committed, ongoing, and relentless effort to ensure the new culture takes hold is just as useless. In fact, this may be worse than useless. If the staff does not see the leadership team making a significant, uncompromising effort to implement the strategic plans and supporting culture that everyone worked so hard to develop, then it is almost certain that staff morale, productivity, and loyalty will plummet.

Implementation is extremely important, so this section of the book offers guidance and advice for you to successfully implement your organization's new strategic and operational plans as well as your values and new, desired culture.

13

Following up and implementing your strategic and operational plans

A fter your strategic planning retreat, final planning activities by staff should be completed within one to two weeks and involve everyone in the different departments or teams. Staff members who are responsible for implementation need to be involved in making their plans. Otherwise, the quality of planning will be lower and their commitment will be diminished, since their expertise and experience are needed in the planning as well as in the implementation.

Here is a helpful tip: I find it most productive if all departments in an organization dedicate the same day or days to complete the plans. When one department finds that it will need support, input, or action by another department, it communicates this, so the other department can include that support, input, or action in its respective plan. Everyone is there to help, and everyone finishes together.

Preparing the final strategic plan and operational plans

Steps after the strategic planning retreat are:

1. Present the strategic plan and department operational plans to all the staff (including research results and stakeholder analysis). This will inform and involve those who did not participate in the retreat.

A Good Strategic Plan

1.	Vision	Our ideal world
2.	Mission	What we do
3.	Core Values	Our fundamental beliefs
4.	Strategic Goals	What we must achieve
5.	Strategies	How we move forward
6.	Strategic Positioning	What makes us special
7.	Credibility	Why we can be trusted
8.	Organization Culture	How we behave
9.	Objectives for each unit	Exactly where we want to be
10.	Background (what we did)	Research, analysis, assessments

2. Establish a clear deadline to complete or refine all operational plans. All planning should be completed within a specific time after the retreat, for example, one to two weeks.

3. Complete any supporting plans, as needed, and add more details as desired.

4. Have individuals within each department and any interdepartmental teams complete their own appropriate operational plans to support the goals and objectives, following the format in Chapter 9.

5. Complete the values and culture work with all staff involved if you have not yet done so. Implementation of the new culture should have its own detailed operational plan that is shared with all staff.

6. Review all the operational plans to assure they are challenging yet achievable as well as complementary and synergistic.

- Supervisors, department directors, and then top management review the draft operational plans to assure they are complete, comprehensive, compatible, and coherent as well as synergistic and stretching.
- The executive director provides input, guidance, encouragement, and limitations for specific plans.
- The finance director has been providing budgetary input throughout the process to all managers and reviews the final plans as well.
- The fundraising director reviews and elaborates on the plans for fundraising and for support needed from other departments.
- Human resources reviews the plans concerning personnel and staffing.

7. Make certain you have sufficiently covered the following organizational issues:
    - Monitoring and evaluation – Should you create or strengthen the monitoring and evaluation team or identify others who are responsible? How does this unit relate to all other departments? Who is responsible?
    - Learning and development – Should you create or strengthen the learning and development component of your organization? Who is responsible?
    - Training needs and plans – How do you assure an adequate level of skills and experience among staff, both current and new, to achieve objectives? Who is responsible?
    - Individual performance, roles, and responsibilities – How do you assure effective and efficient individual performance? Who is responsible?

- Management performance, roles, and responsibilities – How do you assure effective and efficient management planning, performance, and review? Who is responsible?

8. Produce a final plan and budget. The executive director, finance director, and department heads review the plans, projected revenues, and allocation of expenditures. Operational plans now include objectives, activities, responsibilities, timeframes, progress indicators, reporting, supervision and monitoring, staffing, and budgets. With guidance from top management, the fundraising director makes final projections of revenues, and the finance director prepares the final proposed budget.

9. Put in place a system for periodic appreciation of outstanding effort and achievement and an annual review of staff performance with appropriate rewards, based on the clear plans, measurable objectives, progress indicators, and new culture.

In a comprehensive review at the end of the process, you should revisit, reconsider, and revise previous conclusions to ensure the completed operational plans fit together well.

The board of directors must approve the strategic plan, operational plans, and budgets

The last step is to secure board approval. If you have done your work with the board of directors, they will have endorsed the planning process in advance, provided input into the planning, and participated to some extent in the planning activities.

Actions for the board include:

1. Approve the strategic plan.
2. Approve any major new strategies and program initiatives.
3. Approve the annual topline operational objectives and budgets for all departments.
4. Review and assure a high standard of behavior and ethics throughout the organization.

The board should also periodically:

1. Review and assure compliance with all legal and financial requirements.
2. Review and assure program and other evaluations are effectively conducted and used.
3. Review the performance, roles, and responsibilities of the executive leadership.
4. Consider and develop plans for staff leadership and development.
5. Review the performance, roles, and responsibilities of the board of directors and its committees.

Board strengthening

As indicated above, the board of directors needs to consider its own leadership and development. The board should therefore complete *its own board development plan* for the coming one to three years with input from the executive director.

I find it most effective for board members to address their own plans after they have seen and approved the plans for the organization. As a consultant in this situation, just after the board of directors approves the strategic plan, topline operational plan, and budget for the year, I would say, "And dear board members, it is now time for you to address your own strengthening. What is needed at the board level to achieve your organization's goals and objectives? Is it new skills and experience? New members? New subcommittees? New policies? A new honorary board?" I would then add, "It will give further confidence and encouragement to staff to see that you too are doing your part to achieve the development and results anticipated. I am here to help." Of course, I would have discussed this with the board chair before that meeting.

Asking the board to plan for its own development before the staff has done their work is less likely to generate enthusiasm. With the plans for the year now approved, it is only logical that the board needs to plan for itself as well.

Implementing the strategic plan and operational plans (to be top of mind every day)

The strategic plan's key points are distilled and edited into a strategic communications document to guide staff, board members, and volunteers in their work and to inform and excite external stakeholders. The published plan should flow smoothly from the reader's viewpoint: your name, logo, positioning, and slogan (who you are), vision and mission (why and what you do), values and culture (your beliefs and behavior), accountability and ethics (why you can trust this organization), strategic goals (what you want to achieve), and key strategies (how you will do it).

You can also turn your history, SWOT analysis, and research findings into a section emphasizing your accomplishments, strengths, and opportunities, and (if you are brave) something about the weaknesses you are correcting and the threats you will overcome.

It is vital that you share, and share again many times, your new strategic communications document with staff, board members, volunteers, and other important stakeholders to ensure your strategy stays top of mind, so everyone will continually take steps to implement it.

I have seen all too many plans that looked good, theoretically, at the strategic level but fail at the operational level. Why? Strategy without execution is doomed. Strategy without leadership is forgotten.

Steve Sookikian, communications officer at the Scleroderma Foundation, recently wrote to me with his insights about the importance of active leadership when it comes to living the organization's values and culture: "Many a time throughout my more than 30 years in the nonprofit sector, I have thought back to my experience working with Ken at PLAN and reflected on the positive culture of mutual support and shared goals. It's common for organizations to create lists of values for their employees to follow. It's uncommon for those values to be second nature, and that only happens when you have effective leadership that models the behavior they expect from others."

What is needed to move the planning process forward to success? Yes, top leadership is important, but my experience is that everyone has to be responsible to lead and implement their operational plans successfully and to support others as well. The implementation stage is very much like a sports team. The plan, the coach, and the training are all important, but success comes from every member of the team playing his or her role well, supporting others, and striving to excel in what they do. Leadership, management, and planning are essential – but individual performance wins the game.

Summary: Your strategic plan and operational plans

The final plans motivate and guide staff, board members, volunteers, and other stakeholders.

1. Who we are (name, logo, positioning, and slogan)
2. Our vision and mission statements
3. Our values and culture
4. Our accountability and trustworthiness
5. Our strategic goals and key strategies
6. Summary of annual objectives for all departments – grouped under each strategic goal
7. Overall budget of revenues and expenditures

Summary: Implementation steps for operational plans

1. Produce and disseminate the approved plans to everyone in the organization and to others.
2. Communicate vision, mission, and values frequently as inspiring and motivating messages.
3. Let your strong values strengthen programs, advocacy and communications.
4. Encourage everyone to be looking for improvements in their daily work.
5. Focus on getting the desired culture in place.
6. Pay close attention to progress indicators.
7. Manage the process on a regular basis.
8. Revise operational plans as needed.
9. Learn from each other and others.
10. Celebrate progress and success.

Mid-term review

A well-managed organization conducts a substantive review of the strategic plan at the mid-term – usually about halfway into a three-year or five-year plan. The review considers progress made, objectives achieved or not achieved, and the reasons why. It looks at new opportunities or threats that have arisen, considers internal problems that need to be addressed, and addresses other issues to determine what to do about them. Based on the review, an abbreviated planning process is put in place to respond and prepare for the remainder of the plan period. Of course, significant changes in the environment warrant revisiting and adjusting the plan at any time.

As you get near the end of one year's operational plan, you begin the process of planning for the following year. Organizations find that the planning gets so much easier as they gain experience in the planning and implementing processes.

As I noted earlier in this book, your strategic plan (as well as each operational plan) should not be a hefty, burdensome document. On the contrary, statements should be to-the-point, and the entire plan can be surprisingly brief – even for a large organization. As an example, here is a concise strategic plan for a small community organization, created shortly after the nonprofit was founded. It took just a few well-organized evening meetings to develop and confirm support for the organization's strategic directions.

GreeningRozzie strategic plan

GreeningRozzie was created by a group of residents who believe that Roslindale, Massachusetts, is a perfect community to pioneer innovative and involving community activities to improve our environment, reduce our impact on global warming, and ensure a greener world for our children and grandchildren.

Vision – What it means to be green
Our vision for Roslindale is a community with shade trees on every street, gardens and compost bins in every yard, and rapidly growing consumption of nutritious local foods in homes, restaurants, and schools.

Introduction. We want to help people save money and energy through more energy-efficient housing and businesses, less traffic, and more biking and walking. We want to find ways to reduce waste, toxins, and pollution in homes, restaurants, businesses, and public spaces. We see a community where residents are advocating for greener practices by local restaurants and businesses and holding our elected leaders accountable for a greener Roslindale. We want to involve children and youth, parents and seniors, schools and organizations, and media and businesses to contribute to a greener, more sustainable, and more cohesive community.

Mission – What we do and what we want to achieve
Our mission is to make Roslindale a greener, cleaner, and more cohesive community by working together to promote and implement grassroots projects and activities.

GreeningRozzie will carry out its mission within the following framework:

1. Trees and green spaces – Increased diversity and environmental quality of green spaces; more street trees, green roofs, eco-lawns, orchards, and parks
2. Local food and gardens – Home and community gardens; home and community composting; local farms and markets; potlucks and food preservation
3. Energy efficiency – Energy efficiency and alternative energy sources in homes, businesses, and government offices
4. Efficient transportation – Accessible and efficient systems; increased walking, biking, ride-sharing, and public transit; reduced car use
5. Healthy homes – Use of green products; reduction of environmental hazards and toxins; improved indoor air quality
6. Waste reduction – Trash and litter reduction; increased composting, recycling, and reuse; reduced packaging; reduced consumption; barter and exchange
7. Water conservation – Water re-use and recycling; rain barrels; water run-off management
8. Information and advocacy – Individual and community awareness and action; involvement of residents, schools, businesses, organizations, and neighborhood associations; measurement of energy use, recycling, and other sustainable and unsustainable activities

Identity

We are a community that cares about the people who live here, the space we live in, the larger city of Boston, and the future we create day by day. Together we can plan our future by improving our living space and the way we live, so people can play, work, and learn together in an environment that is healthy for individuals, families, and the community. We seek to include everyone who lives, works, and cares about Roslindale and to draw on its amazing diversity of talents and backgrounds for ideas, skills, commitment, and effort to make it a sustainable green community. We will seek to build momentum through innovation, partnering with others, and welcoming new ideas and new participants.

Board-approved goals

1. The overriding goal of GreeningRozzie is to help achieve a 25 percent reduction in Roslindale's carbon emissions from 1990 levels by 2020-25
2. Goals will be set for each of the eight activity areas
3. Objectives will be established for each project in each activity area
4. Specific metrics to measure progress will be proposed by the metrics taskforce

Priority projects for the upcoming year

1. Home energy efficiency
2. Trees and green spaces
3. Local food and gardens
4. Waste reduction

Organization priorities
1. Nurture the many people already involved in GreeningRozzie
2. Reach out to get more people involved and increase diversity
3. Recruit more leadership for more action
4. Plan next year's projects with clear objectives, focus, and a simple set of actions
5. Link activities to policy and connect with bigger organizations and government
6. Generate funding for support, supplies, and activities

Questions for implementation

1. Is your board of directors "on board" with your strategic planning activities, so they are more likely to be enthusiastic and supportive of the plans as you go through the year?

2. Have you scheduled a day (or days) for all functional areas to work on their plans simultaneously, since this can enhance cross-departmental communication, increase ownership in shared goals, and encourage team members to identify realistic (yet stretching) objectives?

3. Do you have a process in place for each functional area (for example, fundraising, program, and finance/administration) to implement and monitor its operational plans after the strategic planning?

"We have done a great job! Let's celebrate."   *"It was so good working with those of you in other departments!"*

14

Translating values and culture into work

My slogan is "Working together for a better world through strategy, teamwork, and leadership." In this chapter, I want to focus on translating values and culture into more effective work to make a better world.

As presented earlier, it is imperative to identify strong values and the supporting culture you need for success – core values that guide you in everything you do and an inspiring and energized culture that brings everyone together to successfully implement your new strategic plan. An ongoing challenge in implementing your new strategic plan is translating your values and culture into the work you do in all departments. I think most well-functioning nonprofits do quite well in living their vision, mission, and strategies, but bringing values and culture to be front and center in all they do is more challenging.

Getting strong values and new culture in place may be the longest step in your strategic planning

The successful implementation of your new values and culture relies on this fact: Every staff member must gain ownership of the values and culture and incorporate them into their daily plans, thoughts, and actions in order to fully support the strategic plan in everything they do.

Behavior and belief are inside a person's core, so change requires persistence, reinforcement, and encouragement – especially when the new strong values or expectations around the new culture ask people to step up in more assertive ways. For example, an NGO that provides help for refugees would also engage in public education and political advocacy (nonpartisan, of course) in support of refugees. This means your organization would need to confront those who oppose fair treatment of refugees. Many organizations are not accustomed to being so vocal in the public space. Some staff may resist "going this far" to step out of their personal comfort zone.

In another example, an organization helping kids in poor areas of a city with tutoring for college preparation would need to confront the mayor, governor, city council, and others about the inequity of school funding based on property taxes and demand the same level of funding that rich suburbs provide for their kids. Some staff may resist this new need to consistently and publicly voice these concerns. Others may resist due to personal issues (perhaps they spent a lot to buy a house in a good school district). In these examples, strong values and supporting culture would lead to significant changes in the organization's way of working – and in the way individuals must now step up within the organization.

Remember, changing an organization's culture means changing the way people behave within the organization and outside of the organization. This is a major organizational change process. Applying *strong* core values in your daily work may involve an even more significant change process. It means relentlessly standing up for what you believe is right.

There will be barriers! People will resist the change! To use a metaphor from earlier in this book: When the train is ready to leave the station, it is vital that everyone has the chance to get on it.

It will take time and persistence to get everyone on board, much more so than allowing people to work as they have in the past. But everyone will be aiming at the higher levels of progress embodied in your vision and mission.

Early in my career, my work focused on responding to the conditions of poverty that people faced in their daily lives. Clearly, this is important. Yet I came to see that addressing the causes of poverty would, in the long run, be more effective than addressing the symptoms. How can an organization address symptoms as well as the root causes? *By translating your values and culture into your work, your nonprofit can engage at a higher, more strategic level – and move to a higher level of performance with a greater impact on society.*

Here is a good example: An organization focusing on African wildlife knew that poaching was a significant problem. It was nearly impossible to stop poaching until the organization learned that hiring a team of local people to protect wildlife worked better than bringing in outsiders. Why? Because it resulted in more local employment and increased local ownership in the issue. It also encouraged environmentally based tourism, which fueled the local economy. This organization adjusted their strategy from addressing a symptom to finding a solution with multiple benefits and beneficiaries – and a greater impact on society.

Strong values are essential to power your programs, advocacy, and public communications

Promotion of your cause, public education about your cause, and advocacy to support your cause are basic attributes of a nonprofit. Strong core values will activate your organization's non-negotiable beliefs through ongoing and new promotion, education, and advocacy campaigns as well as strengthening program services.

Other fundamental attributes of nonprofits – maintaining your independence and free voice and maintaining your voluntary nature

– are also essential as you translate values into work. You need to have the freedom of speech and strength of your conviction (values) to speak out, even when it may be controversial or unpopular, because you believe it is right and important. If you are supported through voluntary contributions, you have a higher credibility than if you are funded by a special interest group.

In addition, I urge you to take your values and culture out of the office and into the programs you deliver to your beneficiaries or program participants. For example, I worked with an NGO in Colombia whose core value is "the intrinsic value of the human being, created in the image and likeness of God." They actively and consistently shared this value to inspire disadvantaged teenagers by giving them confidence and belief in themselves based on Christian teaching.

I believe most nonprofits need substantial organizational change to meet the needs in the world today. To do so, they must meet the challenge of improving fundraising results and achieving sustainability (the two challenges most often cited). Organizations will not be able to generate sustainability and the financial revenues they want through cosmetic or tactical changes. Instead, you must go through a process of strategic innovation with many new expectations. Getting values strong and culture right is imperative to make it all work. You will attract more highly committed supporters and increased donations.

Your core values statement and the statement of your new, desired culture should be strong and involving for current and prospective employees. Possibly even more significant, it must also inspire trust and respect by donors, participants, officials, opinion makers, other stakeholders, and even those who disagree with you!

How a national nonprofit translated values and culture into work

I was asked to guide a major American health nonprofit through a process to revisit their core values, design a new culture, and translate values and culture into their programs. I had facilitated the organization's strategic planning in the past, essentially with the model I present in this book, and the team had continued to use the same planning approach on their own.

Now a few years later and based on significant success, they had an excellent new strategic plan for their extensive national program, but the executive director felt something was missing in how they were working. She wanted their values to be strong and front and center, because they were facing some resistance. She wanted their values to be clear and relevant to their mission.

With a staff of a dozen, we spent two full days addressing this topic. As a first step, participants identified that "Our new challenges are to further our two new programs, diversify funding, appeal to new donor groups, and think and work in new ways." The expected outputs of the retreat were "a clear and agreed values statement, a new organization culture, improved work habits, and operational plans and indicators." *Good start!*

At the end of a lively discussion, they listed their core values as serving the underserved, finding practical solutions based on science, creating systems change, and being open to change. *That set the stage for real change!*

In the next session, they identified their current culture as: committed and hardworking; mission-driven and results oriented; flexible; crisis mentality and firefighting; not communicating enough; not creating synergy, sharing, learning or creativity." Other listed behaviors were even tougher. It was quite a list! But the executive director was open, and she encouraged everyone to focus on making the values and culture work better.

With enthusiasm, the participants identified their core values and new culture. First, their core values – they were passionate about promoting these values in work:

- Serving the underserved, bringing health into housing and housing into health
- Finding practical solutions based on science, experience, and community needs
- Creating systems change, delivering outstanding results
- Showing integrity: being transparent, trustworthy, dependable, and objective
- Being open to new ideas
- Making a great place to work

Second, their new culture statement – they created this culture to further new programs:

- Mission-driven and results oriented
- Committed, enthusiastic, and hardworking
- Creative, innovative, and synergistic
- Respectful, collaborative, and flexible
- Dynamic and learning

It was clear the newly identified values and culture would support their new, stretching goals, strategies, and objectives. The participants were excited about their new culture, but they were worried. The question was, "How do we get this new culture in place?"

Working together in a forthright discussion, management and staff spoke about the lack of time and limited connections, skepticism and opting out, tradition and bureaucracy, and resistance to change.

They summarized negative aspects of their current culture that would present barriers to the new culture with phrases such as "That's how we've always done it" and "We are quick to criticize and resist change."

Desired culture by this national nonprofit	Barriers to the new, desired culture
Our new challenges are to further our two new programs, diversify funding, appeal to new donor groups, and think and work in new ways. Our new, desired culture is: • Mission-driven and results oriented • Committed, enthusiastic, and hardworking • Creative, innovative, and synergistic • Respectful, collaborative, and flexible • Dynamic and learning	As identified by executives and staff working together, the barriers were: • That's how we've always done it! • We are quick to criticize and resist change. • There is a lack of time, and we focus on operations. • We have limited touch points with our constituency. • There is embedded respect for tradition and bureaucracy. • We opt out of the desired culture. • They won't believe us.

Based on this clarity, the group developed a plan of action to address and overcome these barriers. The next part of the plan created a team with responsibility and authority to take action to overcome the barriers in order to instill the new, desired culture.

Working together, participants produced a clear plan to overcome the identified barriers and to translate the values and culture into their program work. They saw their values and culture as essential to their collaborative work, training, and mentoring. *Excellent progress!*

This national nonprofit created a team to support the values and culture, with this plan of action:

Live it first. Demonstrating it will work. Preaching won't.

- We just need to BE collaborative. We need to behave the way we want to.
- We publicize the culture, post it, and talk about it – remember it!
- We use everything and every touchpoint to demonstrate, drive, and reinforce it.
- We have three steps: We live it. We communicate it. We steer stakeholders to it.
- We do a culture check: Did you do it? Did we live it? We all track ourselves.
- We build it into monthly reviews and discussions.

Create a space to co-create the culture with others.

- We are mentoring leaders of our partners in how we want all of us to behave.
- This is what you can expect from me. Hold me accountable. We expect it of you.
- Expect everyone who becomes involved to see this, know this, and live it too.

Create reinforcement rules.

- Talk about it, help people get it, have a buddy system, and update the rules over time.

In the second day, participants focused on "Translating values and culture into work." They wanted to transfer their new values and culture to their clients and partners in order to have greater impact. To do this, they identified these expected outputs, outcomes, and impacts:

- The expected *output* is a better understanding and agreement by everyone regarding how we work together to achieve objectives.
- The expected *outcome* is more efficient and more effective work as a team and, therefore, more productive and more satisfied staff, board, clients, and other stakeholders.
- The expected *impact* is a more efficient and more effective organization working with partners in better ways to achieve greater impact.

Next, the group developed three new campaigns to achieve their strategic plans and reinforce their values and culture with their local and national clients. *Superb result!*

This example shows how the process of translating values and culture into work can lead to significant success. In effect, they translated their values into a strategy to make their program stronger. Years later, I received a note from the executive director that this "planning process helped us become a more healthy, sustainably funded organization and helped me grow as a leader."

Concluding thoughts to consider as you launch a culture process

As you launch your values and culture process, keep in mind these wise words from Dr. Larry Senn, a pioneer in the field of corporate culture, "When an organization is in touch with its culture, its chances of success in changing strategy increase dramatically."

One benefit of my work as a consultant with so many nonprofits is to have close experience with a great variety of organizations and their respective values and cultures – and to see how effective they can be. I encourage you to consider and adapt my model of good culture for an effective NGO as well as my model for a great fundraising and management culture for your organization.

Ken Phillips' model of a good culture for an effective NGO

1. A "can do" attitude in all we do
2. Respect and appreciation for others
3. Responsibility for solutions and improvements
4. Passion for our vision and commitment to our mission
5. Aiming high with big ideas and continuous improvement

Ken Phillips' model for a great fundraising and management culture

1. Everyone supports the fundraising effort. ("It's my job!")
2. We understand fundraising and have a strong fundraising culture.
3. We increase our efforts and budget to increase fundraising results.
4. We know fundraising is a long-term investment for increased funding.

5. We build capacity of board members, executives, and staff for fundraising.

6. We support leadership initiatives at all levels.

7. We strive to achieve excellence in everything we do.

8. We are solutions oriented and reject problem thinking.

9. We are positive thinkers and are passionate about our vision and mission.

10. We focus on doing the important tasks rather than urgent tasks in our daily work.

Questions for implementation

1. Have you decided how best to do your work to create a new, desired culture as an activity during the strategic planning retreat – or as a separate half-day or full-day session to involve as many staff as possible?

2. How can you use your strong values and supporting culture to be more effective or more powerful in your program, education, and advocacy?

3. Have you downloaded the toolkit "Assessing Your Core Values and Organization Culture" from www.NGOFutures.com to review and use in the planning?

15

Concluding thoughts to make a better world

Now that you are finishing this book, you are ready to commence your strategic planning process. This chapter provides a quick review, a bit more guidance and, I hope, additional inspiration!

Important reminders about the strategic planning process

You probably know where you want to get in the near future, but you need to work with others to define the key elements of your plan to get there. The essential elements are your vision, mission, values, goals, strategies, and culture – these largely define who you are and how you will proceed.

Supporting these are your key strategies that answer these questions:

- How does your program operate? Innovative and effective?

- Who are you in the marketplace? Unique and appealing?

- Why should people trust you? Responsible and accountable?

- How will you proceed in your fundraising? Professional and supported?

Good planning requires *research* to understand the current reality you face and *visioning* to see what you could achieve. The combination of *realism* and *optimism* is what leads to a successful strategic plan.

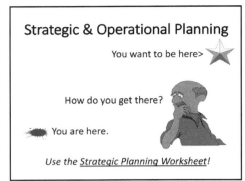

Strategic & Operational Planning

You want to be here>

How do you get there?

You are here.

Use the Strategic Planning Worksheet!

All nonprofit organizations need a good strategic plan, strong values, and supporting culture. You need to involve people in developing that plan, so they will be inspired and committed. Do that well, and you will get the results you want.

The need to have a supporting culture

Organizations may have the topline elements of their strategic plan, but they might neglect or rush to complete the component addressing organization culture. The culture will facilitate your plan if it is the right culture – or undercut your plan (or even sabotage it) if it is the wrong culture. How do you know if you have the right culture? Oil or sand? Examine it, analyze it, and improve it.

Culture at Foster Parents Plan

- Identifying and creating a "can do" culture
  - Passion for the Mission
  - Obsession with Growth
  - Commitment to Customer Service
  - Let everyone shine
- Good results
  - 30,000 donors to 100,000 donors
  - $10 to $30 million income
  - 100 staff to 75 staff

Encourage leadership at all levels

Let me share a few lessons from my first book about leadership and fundraising. If you have read this book (*Make a Better World: A practical guide to leadership and fundraising success*), the following paragraphs serve as a review. If you have not read it, these thoughts may provide inspiration to delve more deeply into the importance of leadership.

Good planning along with empowered leadership and better fundraising are the most needed improvements for most nonprofits. Allowing leadership to flourish at all levels helps the organization do better and achieve more. I advocate an organization culture that encourages leadership at all levels, because I have seen again and again that leadership when you are not "the boss" does miracles in a nonprofit, whether it is struggling or thriving. *Confident leaders welcome leadership initiatives by others.*

Leadership opportunities can be open for everyone in an organization. It just takes initiative to step up and lead when you see a particular issue that needs addressing. Leadership by the fundraising director, the field worker, the accountant, the personnel officer, and everyone else will make a better organization. *It's for you, it's for your colleagues, and it's for a better world.*

Remember these simple steps to leadership

It takes these six simple steps to be a leader:

1. Network everywhere within your organization and externally, so you have partners and supporters.
2. Keep your eyes open all the time to see what needs to be done to improve your work and results.
3. Seize the opportunity when you see something that needs to be improved.
4. Don't let it pass by but actually step up, even when it is awkward and initially controversial.
5. Persist because, certainly, you will encounter barriers and objections as you step up to do something better.
6. Run all your meetings well. (Running meetings well gets results whether the meetings are key board sessions, formal planning retreats, small group work, or chance conversations at the watercooler.)

The greatest leaders throughout history are unique. But they are not us, and we certainly are not them. You can have significant impact in making this a better world by stepping up to lead small and medium improvements – possibly big ones – in your daily work, in your volunteer activities, in your neighborhood or school, and even in your family. You develop your leadership by practicing your leadership. Although mentors, courses, and books are helpful as guides, in the final analysis you have to do it yourself. Remember: *You learn leadership by doing leadership.*

Fundamentals for leaders

With good character – motivated by values and caring and guided by the strategic planning goals – wherever you are in an organization, you can start leading from now. Effective and efficient nonprofits have a culture in which everyone can and should play a role in identifying and resolving issues or problems to make their organization better.

Whether you are a department director, an assistant in the fundraising department, a field worker, someone in the finance office, or work somewhere else in the organization, I know you can make a difference by stepping up. Even if dispersed leadership is not in the current culture, it is well worth the risk for you personally and for the organization for you to break the barriers and step up to the opportunity. *You will stand out! You will make a difference!*

Dispersed leadership enables everyone to contribute to a better organization. The opportunity for leadership is there for the taking. Don't miss the opportunity.

If you are the boss and you are not encouraging leadership at all levels, you could do more. When you open up to more leadership from others, your organization will thrive.

The planning challenge

In my work, I am in contact with many students and young NGO workers. I find it surprising that they don't do much planning. They tell me that, growing up, everything came at them from parents. At the university, everything came at them from professors or administrators. And in many organizations, plans come at them from managers. Unfortunately, what they think is "planning" is actually responding to what is happening or what they are told to do. This approach is reacting rather than initiating. It is short-sighted, ad hoc, and limited. In fact, it is not planning at all. Note the synonyms for planning: *preparing, researching, innovating, organizing, designing, drafting,* and *setting up*. Additional words related to planning activities include *forethought* and *groundwork*.

For many people, the process of planning is actually a new skill and a new way of thinking. It is no wonder that, according to research, so many small and medium-size nonprofits do not have meaningful plans for their future. When I was first doing strategic planning in the United States many decades ago and then teaching it in Eastern and Central Europe and other countries, I would find that most nonprofit organizations did not have clear strategic plans. Near the end of one workshop, for example, I was roasted by participants from Hungary for my optimism about planning for a better future – then they got to work and began to do exactly that.

The best organizations are following this strategic planning process – and getting results and growing

I recall author Peter Drucker saying years ago that nonprofits needed to adopt many of the techniques and methods of management found in the best-performing companies. He was right. The good news is that in the United States and more recently in other countries, there has been a revolution in management at the best nonprofit organizations. I was so happy, for example, a few years ago when I attended a conference in Washington, D.C., with large and sophisticated NGOs and learned that they were adept in their planning, their cultures, their strategies, their management, and their state-of-the-art planning processes.

Well-formulated strategic plans, well-drafted operational plans, and well-defined organization culture are now hallmarks of the best-performing nonprofits around the world. But these are the exceptions – the big, sophisticated, professional, and well-managed nonprofit organizations. *And the best nonprofits are growing bigger and faster!*

Nonprofit organizations in most countries are achieving impacts that do make a better world, and this is a result of their inspiring visions, motivating missions, effective management, and values and culture that facilitate achievement. Their accomplishments come from melding optimism and reality, engaging staff and volunteers, and encouraging leadership at all levels. *But they can do so much better with careful planning!*

Most nonprofit organizations need to step up

Although progress in the sector has been substantial, strategic planning does not appear to be a priority for many organizations. Think about the recent research that found more than half of all nonprofits surveyed did not have a strategic plan at all or did not have one that they were using. This statistic certainly understates the problem, since organizations that are new, small, or really struggling were less likely to be included in the research findings. I estimate that up to a quarter more may have plans that they are following, but their plans have not been well constructed.

All nonprofits – and I mean 100 percent of nonprofit organizations – *need to prioritize planning as essential strategy.* Nothing can be more important than this! It is about what you want to achieve in the world. It involves forward thinking, identifying where you want to be, working back to the present, and deciding what activities are needed to achieve the results you want. Your donors expect it, your program participants or beneficiaries need it, and your staff and volunteers are eager for it. Planning involves *preparing, researching, innovating, organizing, designing, drafting,* and *setting up.* It involves *forethought* and *groundwork.* It is not that hard to do, and now you can do it.

Learning about planning is generally not taught in schools (other than in project planning courses). But the needed planning guidance is right here in this book, ready for you to use.

Planning can be easy and fun

Planning is not that difficult. Regardless of the size and complexity of your organization, you can make it easy to do. Each time you engage in strategic and operational planning, it gets easier to do. It becomes normal and standard. *You can do it!*

Once they are involved, people want to help determine their plans and their activities. You will find that planning together creates a closer team, more cooperation, and amazing synergy. When they are involved, people will look forward to the planning sessions, want to make improvements, and are determined to help the organization grow and accomplish more.

Large and complex organizations have many people who can effectively lead, support, and enjoy the process. Smaller and less complex organizations can complete the research and planning in a simpler process and reasonably short time. A community organization can develop a meaningful strategic plan, annual plan, and culture in just a few evening meetings.

Do enough research to know you are grounded in reality. Do enough brainstorming and visioning to be confident you have stretched your thinking. Spend as much time as you need to identify or update your vision, mission, and values as the foundation of everything you do. Get people involved in developing their own plans, activities, and responsibilities to implement the mission and progress toward the vision. Develop your culture as an expression of your values and support for their plans. These are exciting and rewarding activities in an organization.

All of this involves change. To make change management smooth, don't talk about change. Instead, focus on these four key steps:

1. Lead with the vision everyone agreed.
2. Focus on the results everyone planned.
3. Communicate frequently that you will succeed.
4. Work together through strategy, teamwork, and leadership.

Wherever you are in the organization, you can help others know what to do. Do what you need to do, so you can do it well. You can change the world! Good luck. Or rather, as I prefer to say: Have courage. Celebrate what you do and who you are!

Go to www.NGOFutures.com for detailed guidance and worksheets on planning and culture to download and use in your planning sessions. And look for the next book in my Civil Society Series: *25 Proven Strategies for Fundraising Success.*

YOU must lead the planning to get results you want!
It is not that hard to do.
You have the tools.

"Hey guys, here's what you need to do!"

Questions for implementation

(whether you are the executive director, fundraising director, other director, other staff, or key volunteer willing to step up)

1. Needed now: What do you need now to get a top-notch strategic plan, operational plan, and culture in place? How will you get all you need?

2. Integrated strategy: How will you guide the planning to get what works best for program results, fundraising growth, and organizational stability?

3. Your leadership: How will you use the vision, mission, values, culture, and plans to inspire others to excel?

4. Shared leadership: Who will you involve as partners in the process? How will you mentor them to step up to new leadership roles?

5. Civil society responsibility: What more can you and your team do to make this a better world?

Appendix 1:
What needs to be done in your strategic plan? – Checklist

Name_____

Organization/Unit_____Date _____

Do we have the following in place? Top rating is 5.	Yes or No?	Rate 1 to 5	What will we do to improve our planning? Action Result Due Date		
1. Energizing vision statement	Yes/No				
2. Empowering mission statement	Yes/No				
3. Strong core values statement	Yes/No				
4. Thorough donor assessment	Yes/No				
5. Insightful competitor analysis	Yes/No				
6. Powerful long-term desired results	Yes/No				
7. Valid SWOT and market analysis	Yes/No				
8. Strategic goals based on critical issues	Yes/No				
9. Memorable strategic positioning statement	Yes/No				

Do we have the following in place? Top rating is 5.	Yes or No?	Rate 1 to 5	What will we do to improve our planning? Action Result Due Date		
10. Strong credibility statement	Yes/No				
11. Unifying organization culture	Yes/No				
12. Strategy for growth of revenues	Yes/No				
13. Strategy for program innovation	Yes/No				
14. Strategy for efficiency and cost control	Yes/No				
15. Strategy for learning and development	Yes/No				
16. Strategy for advocacy and lobbying	Yes/No				
17. Strategy for board development	Yes/No				
18. Annual objectives and plans for all	Yes/No				
19. Clear progress indicators	Yes/No				
20. Annual review	Yes/No				

Appendix 2:
Considerations to prepare for your strategic planning – Checklist

This checklist will help you prepare, implement, and follow up your strategic planning process.

Preparation and authorization

1. Is the executive director committed to engage in a strategic planning process?
2. Does he or she accept that the process may lead to substantial changes and new directions?
3. Does he or she accept that the process may bring up awkward issues at times?
4. Do other senior staff members agree to the above as well?
5. Does the board of directors endorse launching a strategic planning process?
6. Is the board of directors willing to engage in the process?
7. Is it clear that the board of directors has the responsibility to approve the final plan?

The strategic planning organizing team

8. Is there a small organizing team that will shepherd the process?
9. Does the organizing team have the right representation and authority?
10. Has the organizing team determined the process, facilitation, and support for the planning?

Internal or external facilitator/consultant

11. Has there been discussion about managing the planning process and facilitating the retreat?
12. If we need an external consultant/facilitator, have the terms of reference been prepared?
13. Have we engaged in a search to find an experienced consultant to facilitate the process?
14. Has an internal or external consultant/facilitator been selected and involved?
15. Have top leaders had an opportunity to discuss sensitive issues with the consultant?

The strategic planning group (retreat participants)

16. Have we created the strategic planning group to carry out the research tasks needed?
17. Does the strategic planning group have a leader? A facilitator? A reporter?
18. Are all those who will be involved in the planning aware of the process and timetable?
19. Has the executive director communicated the importance of honesty in the assessments?
20. Has a plan of action and timetable been prepared and circulated to all who will be involved?
21. Have we personally invited the individuals who will participate in the planning process?

Research and other preparation

22. Have we prepared a comprehensive list of plans, reports, and other materials to be reviewed?
23. Have we identified the key stakeholders to be interviewed?
24. Have we identified the various stakeholder groups to be surveyed?
25. Have we identified the organizations for the competitor assessments?
26. Have we assigned responsibility for those who will conduct the different research tasks?
27. Have we drafted the questions for these interviews? For the surveys?
28. Have we conducted an assessment of our current planning process and results?
29. Have we invited external experts to talk about the current landscape and the future?

Space and materials

30. Have we organized the meeting place and rooms for full group and small group meetings?
31. Have we organized refreshments and meals and, if needed, accommodations?
32. Have we organized screen and projector, flip charts and markers, pens and paper?
33. Have we organized travel to the facility for the retreat?

Agenda

34. Have we drafted and circulated an agenda with detailed topics to be covered day by day?
35. Have we confirmed those who are doing research will complete their tasks on time?
36. Will we circulate research findings in advance for consideration?
37. Have we confirmed the participants in the retreat?
38. Have we asked people to bring their personal computers for use during the planning?
39. Have we defined the dress code, indicated the expectation to begin on time, and communicated any other requests, suggestions, or helpful information?

Process at the strategic planning retreat itself

40. At the meeting, will we review the agenda, the process to follow, and expected outcomes?
41. Will we assign responsibilities for small-group discussions – leader, facilitator, and reporter?
42. Will we set a standard for plenary and small group discussions to focus on short statements, with active participation by everyone?
43. Will we have a process to allow for needed discussion yet keep the pace moving?
44. Will we allow time for those who conducted research in advance to summarize their findings?
45. Will we assure that one person in each session captures important ideas and conclusions?
46. Will we have a mechanism (PowerPoint projection) to share group reports?
47. Will we have a mechanism (PowerPoint projection) to share and revise draft statements?
48. Will we have a process to resolve or defer for later any contentious or irrelevant issues?
49. As we go through the process, will we review drafts of key items to confirm consensus?
50. Will we be willing to edit previously approved drafts based on new insights?
51. Will we prepare a final draft of the plan with research and working documents as attachments?

After the strategic planning retreat

52. Will we organize needed follow-up activities to complete all plans?
53. Will we conduct meetings with staff to elaborate and reinforce the plan for implementation?
54. Will we organize culture sessions to define the new, desired culture (if we didn't complete this during the retreat)?
55. Will we prepare posters to remind everyone of the vision, mission, culture, positioning, etc.?
56. Will we give the final draft of the strategic plan to the board for approval?
57. Will we circulate the final, approved strategic plan to all staff and volunteers?
58. Will we publicize the plan to key stakeholders?
59. Will we keep the plan on everyone's desk as a living document to reinforce its implementation?

Appendix 3:
Agenda for a three-day strategic planning retreat – Template

Participants (list names and responsibility): _____

Location (specify address and contact points): _____

Dates (specify latest arrival and earliest departure times): _____

PRELIMINARY DAY: Getting started

1. Arrival no later than 5:00 pm
2. Gathering and reception at 6:00 pm
   a. Welcome and setting the agenda and tone for the meeting – executive director
3. Working dinner and group discussion – 7:00-8:30 pm – facilitator (optional session)
   a. What do we want personally from this meeting? 3-5 individual objectives
   b. What does *our group* want organizationally from this meeting? 3-5 organization objectives
4. Feedback after dinner – 8:30-10:00 pm – facilitator
   a. Feedback on what we want from this meeting, individually and for the organization
   b. The value of strategic planning
      i. Determine the future of the organization
      ii. Clarify for others who we are, what we do, and how we do it
      iii. Create the basis for fundraising and for partnerships
      iv. Work more effectively and efficiently toward our goals
   c. What we will do at this meeting? What are the issues to address? (schedule, details, etc.)

DAY ONE: Taking stock to understand the realities we face and the possibilities we could achieve

1. Breakfast – 8:00-9:00 am
2. **Assessing where we are** – 9:00 am-1:00 pm
   a. Our history: where we come from – executive director (capture key findings in flip charts or PowerPoint slides)

    b. Recent evaluations and reports on what we have achieved – staff as assigned
        i. Annual reports on achievements
        ii. Other substantive reports and evaluations: Lessons learned (capture key findings in flip charts or PowerPoint slides)
    c. Survey results on program participants, donors, partners, authorities, prospects, and staff – staff as assigned (capture key findings in flip charts or PowerPoint slides)
    d. Our competitors and what we learn from them – staff as assigned (capture key findings in flip charts or PowerPoint slides) – staff who compiled the research
    e. Our current donors and what we can learn from them – staff as assigned (capture key findings in flip charts or PowerPoint slides) – staff who compiled the research
    f. Analysis of program director, fundraising director, and finance/administrative director (capture key findings in flip charts or PowerPoint slides) – the directors in turn
    g. Findings and recommendations from the confidential interviews – consultant (capture key findings in flip charts or PowerPoint slides)
    h. How did we do in our current strategic plan? Group discussion and feedback – facilitator
        i. What worked and why
        ii. What did not work and why (capture in flip charts or PowerPoint slides)
3. Working lunch – 1:00-2:00 pm – Review from the outside (the landscape we face) – invited guests (capture key findings in flip charts or PowerPoint slides) – executive director
4. **Where do we want to be** – 2:00-6:00 pm
    a. Dreams and aspirations – What I would love to see us do in the future (visionary session) (capture key findings in flip charts or PowerPoint slides) – facilitator
    b. Donors and other key stakeholders assessment – groups and plenary feedback
        i. Identify main stakeholder groups
        ii. Go to the next level of individuals in the various groups
        iii. Identify what we want from them and what they want from us (capture in flip charts or PowerPoint slides)

   c. Desired long-term results in ten to fifteen years – groups and plenary feedback
      i. Stretching our thinking if we had all the resources we needed
      ii. Results and measurements (capture in flip charts or PowerPoint slides
   d. Discussion of the process so far
5. Reception, dinner, and working groups – 7:00-9:30 pm (optional sessions)
   a. Discussions on program with participants from other departments
   b. Discussions on marketing and fundraising with participants from other departments
   c. Discussions on finance and administration with participants from all departments
   d. Confirming benefits for key stakeholders

DAY TWO: Setting the framework to move forward – drafting the strategic plan

1. Breakfast – 8:00-9:00 am
2. What we will do – 9:00 am-1:00 pm – facilitator
   a. Review of the work so far and feedback from working groups (capture in flip charts or PowerPoint slides)
   b. Draft our vision – groups and plenary consensus (capture in flip charts or PowerPoint slides)
   c. Draft our mission – groups and plenary consensus (capture in flip charts or PowerPoint slides)
   d. Draft our core values – groups and plenary (capture in flip charts or PowerPoint slides)
   e. Conduct our SWOT – groups and plenary feedback (capture all key findings in flip charts or PowerPoint slides)
      i. Internal strengths and weaknesses
      ii. External opportunities and threats
      iii. Discussion of how to respond to weaknesses, threats, strengths, opportunities
   f. Identify the critical issues we face for the next three to five years – groups and plenary based on the research, stakeholder analysis, SWOT, and all the other information (capture in flip charts or PowerPoint slides)

3. Working lunch – 1:00-2:00 pm
   a. Identify the strategic goals for three to five years (capture in flip charts or PowerPoint slides) – facilitator
4. **How we will proceed** – 2:00-5:00 pm – facilitator
   a. Key strategies – groups and plenary (capture key points for each topic in flip charts or PowerPoint slides), for example:
      i. Innovative program strategy – Why, what, where, how, and who?
      ii. Advocacy and influence strategy – Why, what, where, how, and who?
      iii. Growth strategy – Why, what, where, how, and who?
      iv. Partnership strategy – Why, what, where, how, and who?
      v. Other strategies
         (Note: the strategies on positioning and credibility could be done by two separate groups.)
   b. Draft our strategic positioning – groups and plenary or delegated to internal expert
      i. Name and logo, positioning statement, and slogan (capture in flip charts or PowerPoint slides)
   c. Draft our credibility statement: How to be trusted – groups and plenary or expert group (capture in flip charts or PowerPoint slides)
   d. Assess our organization culture – groups and plenary (deferred to later for large staff) (capture key points for each topic in flip charts or PowerPoint slides) (Alternative to do it later)
      i. Define our current culture
      ii. Define our new, desired culture
      iii. Determine how we will reinforce the new culture
5. Reception, dinner, and working groups – 6:00-10:00 pm (optional sessions)
   a. Financial management working group with participants from other departments (optional session)
   b. Communications working group with participants from various departments (optional session)
   c. Capacity building working group with various participants (optional session)

DAY THREE: Establishing what we will actually do – drafting and implementing operational plans

1. Breakfast – 8:00-9:00 am
2. **Who we are and what we do** – 9:00 am-1:00 pm – facilitator
   a. Feedback from working groups (capture in flip charts or PowerPoint slides)
   b. Review the key elements of the strategic planning
   c. Clarifying or completing any unfinished work on the Strategic Plan
   d. Brainstorming: Creative session on possible objectives for the coming year (capture in flip charts or PowerPoint slides)
   e. Assignment of draft objectives to departments to refine objectives – executive director
   f. Independent and team or department work to draft operational plans
3. Lunch – 1:00-2:00 pm
4. **Drafting the operational plans for the coming year** – 2:00-6:00 pm
   a. Independent and team or department work to draft operational plans
   b. Connecting to other teams for cooperation needs – plenary
   c. Feedback on topline objectives and any other issues to be addressed – plenary (capture in flip charts or PowerPoint slides)
   d. Agreement on next steps to complete the planning – executive director (capture all key points in flip charts or PowerPoint slides)
      i. Who does what by when after this meeting?
      ii. Documentation of the meeting
      iii. Communication of the outcome
      iv. Projected sources and amounts of revenue
      v. Organizational structure and budget and staffing issues
      vi. Future meetings
5. Reception and celebration – 6:00-7:00 pm

Appendix 4:
How to get detailed worksheets for your planning process

I encourage you to download detailed versions of the worksheets you have seen in this book – along with additional interactive planning tools. These tools are essential for your strategic planning, and they are available free for readers of this book.

The worksheets are tools I developed and refined over many years while consulting with hundreds of nonprofits in dozens of countries. They will guide you, your staff, and other planning participants as you work to create your new plans.

By following the guidance in this book and using these tools, the outcome will be an inspiring strategic plan and dynamic operational plans that empower your organization to build on past achievements, correct weaknesses, and move forward with challenging and stretching plans. Plus, you and your team will create strong core values and a vibrant organization culture that supports your strategic plans and, ultimately, contributes to making a better world.

**Tools for strategic and operational planning –
created by Ken Phillips, NGO Futures LLC**

I. Preliminary Preparation
   Three detailed guides for planning your planning
II. Research and Analysis before the Planning: A Complete Planning Toolkit
   Guidance and ten worksheets for research tasks
III. Developing Key Inputs for Your Plans: A Complete Planning Toolkit
   Guidance and four worksheets for work in innovative thinking

These tools are designed to guide and assist nonprofit organizations, community associations, and groups in formation in drafting their own plans and strategies.

These tools are available as Microsoft Word documents to facilitate your sharing and enable you to use them on my website (www.NGO-Futures.com). I encourage you to download them and use them interactively and expansively in your meetings. Smaller NGOs and community groups can simplify these tools, so the planning process can be completed in several half-day meetings or several evening sessions. Go to www.NGOFutures.com.

About the Author

Backed by fifty-five years of leadership in the NGO sector, Ken Phillips has earned respect around the globe for his expertise on strategy, teamwork, and leadership. His writing is based on twenty-five years of practical experience actually leading and managing nonprofits and thirty years of consulting and training in strategic planning, fundraising, and organizational development with hundreds of organizations in the United States, Eastern Europe, and other regions. Ken's insights are strategic, practical, and proven. Simultaneously, he inspires and energizes nonprofit workers and volunteers, reminding them that they are making this a better world.

In his first leadership position, Ken served as president of AIESEC-US, an international student-run organization exchanging students for international internships. He increased the exchanges and revenues by 50 percent in two years. He then served as coordinator of planning and project development at the Institute of International Education in New York. Responsible for corporate and foundation fundraising, Ken developed innovative international programs and managed a successful anniversary fundraising campaign ($17.7 million in 2020 dollars).

As vice president of development at Save the Children, Ken developed new core strategies for the organization, diversified the fundraising function, and achieved a doubling of income and a tripling of public awareness. As president and national executive director of Foster Parents Plan, he led a significant change process for the board of directors, established a prestigious honorary board, initiated important educational and advocacy programs, and increased revenues from $10 million to $30 million (the equivalent of about $64 million in 2020 dollars). Simultaneously, he reduced administration costs by 25 percent.

As a member of the board at InterAction, the association of American NGOs working internationally, Ken led the first association-wide strategic planning process, organized a major fundraising study for the sector, successfully advocated support for the Convention on the Rights of the Child, led the creation of InterAction's pioneering Private Voluntary Organization (PVO) Standards, and served for two years as chairman of the board of directors.

While working at the International Federation of Red Cross and Red Crescent Societies in Switzerland, Ken held the position of head of organizational development. While there, he created the theoretical framework, strategies, guidance, and measurements for effective organizational development for its National Societies. This included procedures, tools, and models for staff and consultants to support National Societies in leadership, governance, planning, managing, finance, fundraising, programming, volunteers, youth, community development, and capacity building.

As a volunteer, Ken led a neighborhood association in Providence, Rhode Island, and an environmental association in Boston, Massachusetts, to record achievements, both times receiving the mayor's award for best community or environmental organization in the city.

He was elected to the Rhode Island Constitutional Convention in 1986 where he served as secretary of the Committee on Ethics, which drafted a powerful non-political Ethics Commission with subpoena power for all elected and appointed officials at the state and city levels. Approved by the electorate, the Commission dramatically reduced corruption in the state.

In 1995, Ken established his consulting firm NGO Futures Sàrl in Geneva, Switzerland. Later, he recreated this as NGO Futures LLC in the United States. His consulting practice, then as today, provides analytical studies to determine needs and action as well as consulting and training workshops in strategic planning, organizational development, fundraising strategies, and board strengthening. His focus is guiding nonprofit organizations to financial sustainability, fostering their organizational development and capacity building, facilitating strategic and operational planning, and mentoring senior executives and board members in leadership and governance.

In addition to consulting with a variety of national and international organizations, Ken has been a frequent presenter at conferences in cities around the world including Greater Boston, Bucharest, Geneva, Kyiv, Moscow, New York, Prague, Vienna, Washington, D.C., Warsaw, and various Internet platforms.

Ken holds an undergraduate degree from Princeton University, a master's degree in literature from the University of Michigan, and a master's degree in economics from New York University. He resides in Boston with his wife Rebecca and is the proud father of three and grandfather of five.

A key theme throughout Ken's entire working career – and in his personal life – is his commitment to guiding and inspiring everyone to make this a better world by creating a more civil society. His books in the *Civil Society Series* and other writings address critical components of organizational capacity building that are needed to support leadership and fundraising efforts in nonprofit organizations. In addition to the guidance on strategic and operational planning, values, and culture presented in this book, the series covers leadership development and fundamental fundraising principles; proven strategies for fundraising success; ethics and learning to gain the trust of donors and the public;  governance, management, and teams working together for results; and advocating to strengthen civil society and the culture of philanthropy in your city and country. In 2019, Ken received the prestigious Peacemaker Award from the global AIESEC Alumni Association.

For further information and updates from Ken Phillips, go to www.NGOFutures.com.